HAM RADIO FOR

BEGINNERS

The Complete Newbie's Guide to Build & Operate Your

Amateur Radio Station. Includes Preparation Material for

the FCC Technician License Test

Richard Duckstein

Contents

Introduction

Amateur radio is a hobby that involves communication through radio transmitters. Many enthusiasts enjoy communicating with other radio amateurs in different countries and use their radios for emergency help. It is commonly known as radio communication, and those who practice it are called hams or amateurs. The term "ham" stands for "amateur," and a person interested in radio engineering practices it for self-education, mutual contacts, and technical research. Many people also use their amateur radios for entertainment purposes. The work of an amateur radio communication service is done without the aim of extracting material gain and with official permission.

Radio amateurs design transceiver radio equipment and antennas and establish radio communications with each other. In radio communication, they can conduct various studies and experiments and exchange information of mutual interest. Often, radio amateurs also compete in operator skills. Why build your radio stations if today, at any time, you can contact by phone or via the Internet with any part of the Earth? Why do people put on a heavy backpack and walk for a month to where they can fly in an hour? Why do they get up at four in the morning and sit with a fishing rod on the river bank all day when you can buy as many fish as they like in the nearest store? Because they are interested because they enjoy not only the result but also the process. This is the process of cognition, technical creativity, sports passion, and the collector's enthusiasm. Contacting any point on the Earth via the Internet or telephone is far from always possible. But if there is a radio amateur there, you can go.

Who Can Become A Radio Amateur?

Any person, regardless of age, gender, or education. The only requirement is to successfully pass the relevant exam and obtain official permission (license) from the Communications Administration of your country to install and operate an amateur transceiver radio station.

Those who have acquired sufficient initial training, but do not yet have an individual license, may be admitted to work on community amateur radio stations for educational purposes under the direct supervision of responsible persons. There are a variety of people among radio amateurs - schoolchildren, academics, peasants, heads of state, homemakers, astronauts, and priests

How I Adopted The Hobby Of Ham Radio?

The hobby began with a trip to the local club, which had a radio school, a radio club, and a collective radio station. There, I became interested in the versatility of amateur communications on HF waves. This is just working on the air, hunting for DX stations (rare and distant), monitoring the work of radio expeditions, and participating in competitions. And just the opportunity to contact different continents of the globe. Just the thought of such a possibility stirred my imagination.

The categories of shortwave radio amateurs are divided into two large groups - those who conduct radio communication sessions (QSO) and observers. To get acquainted with radio communications, it is easier to start with observations, gain experience, study how experienced radio amateurs work, and comprehend radio communication etiquette.

Looking ahead, I'll say that my passion for HF communications, the practice of a radio operator, and the study of the design of transceiver equipment and antenna facilities gave me invaluable knowledge that helped me a lot while serving in the Armed Forces in the communications unit.

Generally speaking, radiosport implies several areas: sports telegraphy, sports radio direction finding ("fox hunting"), all-around radio operators, and radio communications on HF and VHF.

Chapter 1: Let's Start With Ham Radio

The History Of Ham Radio

I think history could not save the name of the first radio amateur. After all, the experiments carried out "for themselves" carried away by reports of wireless telegraphy were not recorded. As a rule, only relatives and friends of such a home experimenter knew about them. One of the first amateurs was the Slovak priest Josef Murgash. In 1896, he emigrated to the USA and became interested in the nascent radio, equipped with a home laboratory, where he reproduced experiments on radio telegraphy. Murgash's inquisitive mind suggested reducing the radio transmission time of telegraph messages in Morse code. He proposed transmitting "dots" and "dashes" in parcels of the same, very short duration but different frequencies. Murgash filed two applications for this method - in 1903 and 1904, and 1904 received two patents.

Rare in our time, the almost gone concept of "radio amateur" and "HF radio sportsman" some 15-20 years ago was intriguing. Enthusiasts with a soldering iron in their hands dismantled circuits and exchanged ideas and new designs of transceivers. They showed remarkable ingenuity in their search for the necessary radio components in conditions of general shortage

How Far Can Amateur Radio Be Established?

The transmitter's range is determined not so much by its power as by the conditions for the propagation of radio waves (passage). Under favourable conditions for the propagation of an HF transmitter, even a very low power (units and fractions of a watt) can be heard at almost any arbitrarily large distance. For example, on the 21 or 28 MHz bands, communication with Antarctica or Australia with a transmitter power of 10-20 W and a simple antenna is not such a rarity, and communication with American or Japanese radio amateurs is generally a daily routine, especially during the years of maximum solar activity. On VHF, long-range propagation of radio waves is very rare and is usually limited to Europe. Still, with great experience and solid technical equipment, some radio amateurs regularly establish the same long-range communications on VHF and HF (for example, by reflecting radio signals from the Moon). The study of the patterns of the passage of radio waves is one of the interesting and scientifically significant activities of radio amateurs.

How Expensive Is Amateur Radio?

Exactly as much as you can afford. Quite worthy home-made equipment can be independently built from very cheap radio components, then almost all of its cost will consist of the labour you have invested in it.

But even if you have a lot of extra money, spending it all on buying various equipment, antennas, and industrial-made accessories is not difficult. Prices for amateur shortwave transceivers (transceivers) of industrial production (mostly Japanese) range from 600 to 9000 USD, and various HF antennas -

from 200 to 3000 USD. A simple pocket 2m VHF FM transceiver can cost around $150, and a used one can cost half as much.

Is There Any Practical Use For Amateur Radio?

Some of the practical uses of Ham Radio can be described as following:-

1. Introduction to the technical knowledge of young people and, in general, people of various professions.

2. Acquisition of practical skills in handling complex electronic devices.

3. Assistance in providing emergency communications in cases of natural disasters and natural and artificial disasters.

4. Maintaining communication in various non-standard situations (expeditions, rescue activities).

5. Serious technical research and mass scientific experiments.

6. Expanding the general outlook of people with the most diverse levels of education.

7. Strengthening mutual understanding between people.

Can Radio Emissions From An Amateur Transmitter Be Harmful To Health?

Such cases with legal amateur radio transmitters have not been recorded. An ordinary mobile phone is potentially more dangerous, not to mention high-voltage power lines. Unfortunately, in the minds of incompetent laypeople, large antennas are often associated with a threat to health, but these fears have no scientific basis. No antennas alone can affect the state of health (after all, these are just the same metal structures as any others around us). It depends on which radio waves are emitted, with what power, and how often they are used.

Moreover, if radio transmissions are carried out using the antenna, the higher the antenna is installed, the less likely the impact of these transmissions on the environment. The amateur radio station usually does not emit anything since it is at the reception. In those relatively short periods when there is a transmission, the parameters of radio emissions do not reach the limits established by sanitary standards. In any case, however, the safety regulations must be strictly observed.

The Hardware Of A Ham Radio Station

A Ham HF radio station's equipment can consist of separate receiver and transmitter units and a combined device called a transceiver. And also, their combinations are not uncommon, especially when participating in competitions. As a rule, the transceiver is designed for all amateur radio communication bands. It covers the frequency range of 0.1 - 30 MHz, but for beginner radio amateurs, 1-2 band devices will be enough to comprehend the basics. Still, it is desirable to have a multi-band receiver. The frequency of the receiver and transmitter in the transceiver are the same, simplifying operational work in the air.

Amateur equipment can be assembled independently, but this requires the appropriate qualifications of a radio amateur, experience in building devices of this class, and measuring equipment. As in any business, the equipment of the workplace is crucial.

In this regard, the observer only needs a receiver, but sports results depend on its quality and, first of all, the sensitivity of the receiving path. I started with a tube receiver from some military radio station; the apparatus weighed excessively, emphasizing the strength of the army with my armour. Then, taking up a soldering iron, more modern receivers were assembled from the magazines "Radio" and "Radio Amateur," which immediately affected the reception quality.

Equipment And Apparatus

For FM radio, you need to find a room and equip a studio in it. There are no special requirements for the arrangement of rooms; the main thing is to provide appropriate sound insulation to prevent the appearance of noise interference in the air. It will be enough for a small regional radio station to buy an apartment on the top floor of a multi-story building with an area of at least 50 square meters. m. or equip another suitable room.

What is much more important and expensive is the choice of equipment. To install antennas, it is recommended to contact the owners of the towers to agree with them on placement since installing your design with the acquisition of a land plot, supplying power, and directly erecting with further maintenance of this tower will require multimillion-dollar investments. Transmitters are not associated with such costs as inside the radio station. The entire list of other necessary equipment will include the following:

1. Console

2. Recorder

3. Feeder with cable

4. Microphones, headphones

5. Auxiliary equipment

6. Devices for receiving telephone calls and putting them on the air

7. PC, office equipment, software.

This is not the highest quality and most powerful, but the main equipment that should at least be on the radio station. The equipment can vary depending on the employees' qualifications and the radio channel's characteristics. But in any case, the devices must be mounted, connected, and launched by professionals to work smoothly.

What Is Radio Technology?

Heinrich Hertz was the first to demonstrate how the electric and the magnetic field can be used to transmit messages. Back then, in 1886, there were no electron tubes or transistors. The transmission signal was therefore generated using a spark gap. Only later was it discovered that the range of the signals, the radio waves, could be increased with long wires. The spark gap died out, the antenna was born, and the name Funk stayed. And that's why every technical facility that uses electric and magnetic fields to transmit data or communicate is classified as radio technology.

What Is An Antenna?

Simply put, an antenna is a piece of equipment that can both send and receive electromagnetic waves. Its key role is to act as a metallic transducer between a line and free space, allowing for the transmission or reception of signals. Although connected like a two-pole device, its basic structure consists of four poles, two of which are not physically fixed but hang freely in space.

How Are Radio Waves Formed?

Radio waves require a vibration generator to be created; without it, they cannot exist. The generator is typically an oscillator that produces a fundamental or carrier wave, a physical phenomenon. However, in electronics, the term "waves" is not commonly used to refer to radio waves because they are frequencies. The oscillator generates an AC voltage signal with a specific frequency, and when the frequency reaches a certain level, electrical signals tend to radiate into the surrounding space. The frequency is measured in Hertz (Hz), the unit quantifying frequencies.

Basic Components Of A Radiofrequency System

A basic radiofrequency system comprises two essential elements: the radio transmitter or transceiver and the transmission line, which comprises connectors, cables, and an antenna. Transmitters are of all types and applications: data transmission, voice, radio, television, etc.

Each system must meet certain characteristics, such as impedance, signal level, gain, frequency response, and attenuation levels. The radio or transceiver is the one that is responsible for generating or receiving the desired communication. Still, it is necessary to do so through a transmission line comprising cable, connectors, and an antenna.

The cable must be of the best quality possible and designed to operate on radio frequencies, depending on the system to which it has been connected and the weather conditions of the site; There are different types of cables, such as coaxial, LMR, and Heliax, these being the most common, each of them has different loss or attenuation at certain frequencies and length, which is measured in dB/m. The antenna propagates RF energy or radio waves into free space; it is selected based on customer needs, operating frequency, impedance, gain, radiation pattern, size, and cost.

There are directional and omnidirectional grids, parabolic mast reflection, billiard cues, and different materials and gains; the latter is measured in dB (decibels) or dBi (isotropic relative decibels). Do not confuse dB with dBi since there is a difference of 2.15 units; that is, a 4 dB antenna has the same gain as a 6.15 dBi antenna. Many companies express the gains of their equipment in dBi to imply that they have higher gains when that is not true.

The connectors connect the radio, cable, and antenna; there are many types, such as UHF or PL, N, SMA, TNC, BNC, etc. All these with their variants in male, female and reverse, in the same way, it is recommended to select them of the best possible quality since a defective or poor quality connector will cause us problems in our transmission line

How To Make An FM Receiver At Home?

One of the most striking fields for electronics fans is the emission and reception of radio signals. The assembly of a radio receiver is relatively simple as long as we do not demand high sound quality. That is why we propose to assemble a sensitive radio receiver in the commercial band of modulated frequency. Let's do it!

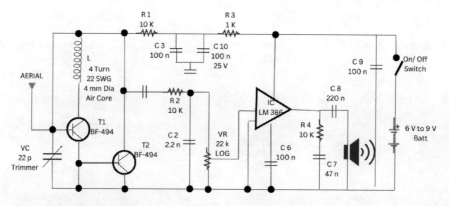

Functioning

In the figure, you can see the reduced scheme of this receiver. The circuit can be divided into two large blocks:-

1. Radio frequency section

2. Low-frequency section

Section Of Radio Frequency

The transistor Q1 and its associated components form the radio frequency section. This transistor is configured as an oscillator/mixer. The capacitor C2 produces positive feedback between the collector and the emitter, producing the oscillation of the transistor at a frequency determined by the tuned circuit formed by L1 and CV. This frequency can be varied by CV and is within the FM band. Capacitors C3 and VR11 produce the oscillation and stoppage of the transistor at a low frequency (not audible) greater than 20Khz. This continuous stop/start produces a situation of the high sensitivity of the transistor to external frequencies of the same value at which it oscillates.

Resistors R1 and R2, and VR1 form the bias network of transistor Q1. Capacitor C1 is responsible for decoupling the positive power supply line. The radio signal captured in the antenna is applied through the step capacitor C4 to the tuned circuit formed by L1 and CV. In this circuit, it is mixed with the signal produced by the oscillator, which is of the same frequency as the captured signal. Therefore, the low frequency (sound) modulated in the radio signal produces a differentiated signal.

To avoid loading the tuned circuit (which would cause null selectivity), the low-frequency signal is obtained from the emitter of Q1. The 1mH L2 coil acts as a high impedance choke before the radio frequency signal, preventing its passage from the emitter to the ground. The audio signal is obtained using a pi filter formed by capacitors C5, C8, and resistor R3. Resistor R4 is in charge of limiting the consumption of Q1 to prevent it from radiating excessive power that would cause interference in nearby receivers.

As you can see, tuning and modulating a radio frequency signal to obtain the audio with a simple oscillator stage is quite easy. As many readers know, this type of receiver is known by the name of "reaction receiver," It has been used since the origins of radio.

Section Of Low Frequency

Once the audio signal is obtained, amplifying it to listen to it in a low-impedance speaker or earphone is necessary. The person in charge of amplifying this signal is the LM386 integrated circuit, which includes a 0.5 w amplifier in just eight pins. The P1 potentiometer is the volume control of our little receiver. Capacitors, while C11 and C10 pass the audio signal and block the DC component. To listen, it is necessary to connect a speaker or headphones between 8 and 32 ohms to the output of the amplifier.

Assembly And Adjustment

To assemble this receiver, a 30w fine tip soldering iron is necessary, as well as 1 mm tin wire and cutting pliers. All the components are very easy to find and cheap. As a circuit board, we recommend making one in fibreglass. However, it may be acceptable to use an island plate like the one used in our laboratory to conduct the tests and adjustments of the prototype. It is not recommended to assemble this circuit on prototype boards (Board) or "line" boards since both have a large capacity between adjacent lines, which causes a malfunction of the receiver. When assembling the circuit, remember to leave plenty of space for the power and ground lines, and solder the components as close to the board as possible (short leads).

The L1 coil can be built by winding four turns of conductive wire on a 0.8mm core. A simple 9v battery pack powers the receiver. Once the assembly is finished, placing the entire circuit with the battery in a metal box that must be electrically connected to the negative power supply (ground) is advisable. This produces a shield that prevents tuning variations and parasitic noise.

You can make a few small holes in the box for tuning and volume adjustments. As an antenna, it is enough with a piece of thread of about 20 cm. Adjustment: The adjustment of the receiver is very simple. Set the volume knob to halfway and adjust VR11 until you hear the typical rattling sound of an untuned receiver coming from the speaker. At that moment, vary the CV condenser until you tune in to a station. If you can't hear anything, try to slightly readjust VR11 or move the turns of L1 apart or together a little.

Improvements: The circuit presented here is valid for the reception of any other signal within the ranges of medium and short waves. Increasing the value of L1 and CV until reaching ten turns in L1 and up to 500 pF for CV is necessary to receive in these bands. The circuit can detect signals regardless of their modulation (FM and AM).

Principle Of The Radio

Radio transmission involves creating a radio wave with a specific frequency and power, modulating it with another frequency carrier, and transmitting it through an antenna. The received signal is then filtered and demodulated to retrieve the originally transmitted signal with some possible differences. Radio frequencies are divided into different ranges based on wavelength and frequency, including long, medium, short, ultrashort, high, extremely high, and hyper-high frequencies.

Radio waves have different characteristics and laws of propagation depending on their frequency range. The ionosphere absorbs long waves (DWs), but ground waves are important for propagation. Short waves (SWs) are absorbed during the day and reflected at night by the ionosphere, creating a radiation zone around the transmitter. VHF waves propagate in a straight line and can bend around obstacles, while HF waves do not and only travel within the line of sight. EHF waves are reflected by most obstacles and used for satellite communications, while hyper-high frequencies behave like light and propagate only within the line of sight. The propagation and characteristics of radio waves vary based on their frequency range.

Chapter 2: Signals & Operations

How Is Data Transmitted By Radio?

While many know that radio communication employs electromagnetic waves to send information into space, there is often confusion about how these waves transmit data. Specifically, people may not understand how radio signals are transmitted and received, particularly about transmitting voice signals. Sound waves travel slowly through the air and quickly decay, making transmitting sound over long distances difficult. However, converting sound into an electrical signal using a microphone makes transmitting the signal over several kilometres or more possible. When someone speaks into a microphone, the voltage outputted by the device changes to match the sound waves. But how can this electrical signal be transmitted over long distances?

By using an antenna, it is possible to release variable electromagnetic waves into the atmosphere. However, the antenna's size must be appropriate to ensure effective radiation of radio waves. Specifically, the length of the antenna must be comparable to the wavelength of the electromagnetic waves to radiate them efficiently. The sound signal's frequency ranges from 20 Hz to 20,000 Hz, with wavelengths spanning from 15 to 15,000 km. Constructing an antenna of this size is a challenging task. As a result, transmitting audio signals directly into the air is not a straightforward process. Even if radiation is emitted, the frequencies of the audio signals broadcast by various stations are nearly identical. Consequently, the signals mix in the air, and the listener cannot select which signal to receive.

In reality, the male voice is less pleasing than the female voice, and female voices are more common. This has led to the idea that, under certain conditions, high frequencies travel farther than low frequencies. To illustrate this concept, scientists compared walking and driving to reach a destination. Walking is slower and requires more physical effort than driving, just as transmitting low-frequency audio signals requires more power and is limited in range. As a solution, different high-frequency electromagnetic waves are generated and used to transmit audio signals via antennas. This allows multiple transmitters to use different frequencies of high-frequency electromagnetic waves without interfering with each other. As a result, relatively small antennas can be designed for this purpose.

The accuracy of this concept has been verified through practical experimentation. The radio transmitter combines several components to produce a synthetic electromagnetic wave transmitted into space via the antenna. Specifically, the transmitter generates high-frequency electromagnetic waves, converts sound and electricity, manages low frequencies, and sends the synthetic wave through the antenna. The high-frequency oscillator produces the high-frequency waves while embedding the audio signal onto the high-frequency vibrational wave is known as modulation. After modulation, the high-frequency vibrational wave is called the "already tuned signal." The modulated signal is then sent to the antenna through a transmission line, allowing it to be radiated and transmitted to a remote location.

The transmitter is responsible for carrying out four primary functions:

1. Converting sound into an electrical signal.

2. Producing high-frequency oscillating waves with a specific power.

3. Utilizing the audio signal to regulate a particular parameter of the high-frequency oscillatory wave is a process known as modulation.

4. Transmitting electromagnetic waves.

To perform the four tasks mentioned above, a transmitter must consist of several components, including a transmitter converter, an RF oscillator, a modulator, an RF amplifier, a transmitting antenna, and a power supply. After transmitting the carrier wave, the receiver's objective is to capture the electromagnetic wave broadcasted in the air and restore it to the original signal.

To receive electromagnetic waves, a receiving antenna is employed. However, since numerous radio stations transmit signals, the antenna receives the desired radio signals and extraneous signals of different frequencies. Radio waves are transmitted using various carrier frequencies to differentiate between the signals. This enables the receiver to "select" the signal it wishes to receive based on the corresponding carrier frequency.

Selective Circuit

The "selective circuit" within a receiver cannot choose a specific electromagnetic wave to receive from a particular station. It is also impossible to directly transfer the signal to the earpiece. The high frequency "imposed" must be eliminated, and the original audio signal must be restored. This process of separating the audio signal from the high-frequency electromagnetic wave is known as demodulation, and the device used for this purpose is called a demodulator. Before the desired signal can be heard, the output audio signal from the demodulator must be sent to the headphones to enable communication.

OOK (On-Off Keying)

OOK (On-Off Keying) is the most basic form of digital coding that involves switching the transmitter on and off by a binary signal. Due to its simplicity, it is widely used in wireless remotes, radio buttons, and other low-cost devices. Typically, no encryption is involved, and the frequency and bit sequence are hardwired, allowing anyone to transmit and receive a signal. As a result, it may not be suitable for use in securing high-value items, such as a Lamborghini parked in a garage. However, it is sufficient for simpler tasks, such as controlling a night light by the bed. For instance, I have been using a night light purchased from a nearby minimart, which employs the OOK principle, for the past three years with no false positives, demonstrating the "elusive Joe" principle in action.

Amplitude modulation (AM)

AM modulation is expected to remain in use for a considerable period, as it is utilized both in broadcast stations and in transmitters operating in the 118-137 MHz air band. One of the unique features of AM is that its spectrum is symmetrical around the central frequency, allowing one to discern whether speech or music is being transmitted roughly. AM was historically one of the earliest methods used for transmitting and receiving speech. The popular "school" detector receiver circuit, which was extremely basic and did not necessitate batteries for reception, utilized the energy from radio waves to power high-impedance headphones. Interestingly, such receivers were mass-produced until the 1960s.

Single sideband modulation (USB, LSB, SSB)

Single sideband modulation, also known as USB, LSB, or SSB, is a unique form of amplitude modulation. In standard AM signals, the spectrum is symmetrical around the center. However, with SSB modulation, only "half" of the signal can be transmitted, providing a greater range for the same amount of transmitter power.

Frequency modulation (FM)

Frequency modulation is the principle behind FM broadcasting, which transmits a complex signal that includes mono and stereo channels, pilot tone, RDS, and more. To distinguish it from "regular" FM, engineers commonly refer to it as WFM (Wide FM). The spectrum of a radio station's signal can be easily viewed using the HDSDR program, revealing the pilot tone at 19 kHz, RDS, mono, and stereo FM broadcast channels. On the other hand, devices like baby monitors and walkie-talkies use "narrow" FM (NFM, Narrow FM) modulation, where the only sound is transmitted. Frequent modulation is also used for digital signals, where a binary code can be transmitted by switching between two frequencies. Even with low power output, radio amateurs can exchange short messages over long distances using FT8. In aviation, an ACARS system combines modulation types by sending digital FM signals via an AM transmitter, likely due to cost savings from utilizing existing equipment.

Phase Modulation (PSK)

In addition to frequency modulation, phase modulation is another way to modify a signal. We can achieve reliable communication over long distances by altering the signal's phase, particularly in satellite communications. Among amateur radio protocols, PSK31 was widely used at one time. With PSK31, a transceiver can be connected to a computer to exchange information through text chat. The number of available phases can vary depending on the speed and communication channel, such as 4, 18, or 16.

Changing a signal's phase and amplitude simultaneously is possible, resulting in even faster transmission, but this requires more complex encoding and decoding. An example of such a signal is QAM. This type of signal can be visualized most easily on a phase plane.

A Simple Shortwave (HF) Receiver For Beginners

We call shortwave radio amateurs who have shortwave radio transmitters and receivers at their disposal. Each amateur radio station has a personal call sign, by which it is possible to determine in which country and even in which region of the country this station is located. Shortwave radio amateurs establish communications with each other and talk to each other using a special international "radio language," or, as it is called, a radio code, which is very simple and quite easy to remember.

With the help of code tables, shortwaves can talk about topics related to their radio equipment and wave propagation and report the most interesting data for any shortwave about the audibility of their radio station and the transmitter quality. Amateur transmitters usually have very low power - no more than 100 watts. Amateurs use narrow sections of the entire shortwave range. These sections of waves are called "amateur bands," located in the sections of the 10-, 14-, 20-, 40-, and 130-meter bands. For example, the amateur 40-meter range covers an area from 41.6 to 42.8 m, and the 20-meter range from 20.8 to 21.4 m.

Using various waves, shortwaves can establish communications over short distances and the most distant communications - for thousands of kilometres. A specially designed receipt card confirms each amateur radio contact. Many radio amateurs have in their collection hundreds and thousands of such receipt cards. Only an experienced radio amateur, who is well acquainted with radio circuits, who knows how to mount and adjust radio equipment and establish radio communications, can build a shortwave radio station.

Building An Amateur Transmitter

To build an amateur transmitter, obtaining a special permit from the Ministry of Communications is necessary, which is issued based on relevant documents. But you can become a shortwave operator without a transmitter by building only one shortwave receiver. There are a lot of such beginner shortwaves in our country. They are called shortwave observers. Observers cannot establish radio contact themselves, but they monitor two-way radio communications of amateur shortwave stations on all amateur bands. To hear about any ultra-long-distance station is no less interesting than to contact it. The work of receiving distant stations is just as exciting as radio communications.

A shortwave observer who has built a shortwave receiver and knows the rules of amateur radio exchange can register his radio installation with a local radio club. He will be given a special certificate indicating the shortwave receiving station's individual "call sign." With such a call sign, a shortwave observer can send receipt cards to all amateur radio stations he hears on his receiver. Each shortwave, having received a card from the observer, sends him his card in response, in which he confirms the receipt of the observer's card and his message about the audibility of the signals of his radio station.

Among the observer cards, one can see a card of a shortwave from the Far East or the Arctic, a card of radio amateurs from Prague Warsaw, and cards of shortwaves of France, Italy, India, Australia, the islands of Oceania, etc. Short-wave radio amateurs work mainly by radiotelegraphy; therefore, to listen to the work of amateur stations, you have to understand how to listen to the telegraphic alphabet, at least at a low speed - only 40-50 letters per minute. Studying the telegraph alphabet in a circle or courses for shortwave radio operators is best.

You can organize a circle to study the reception of the telegraphic alphabet by ear at school or in the House of Pioneers, or even train with a friend in reception by ear and transmission on the key. In extreme cases, you can learn to receive by ear and on your own, listening to the work of radiotelegraph stations on your receiver, but this usually requires much more time and labour.

The detector stage of the receiver is made according to a three-point scheme with an anode grounded at high frequency. The circuit coil is connected to one of the triodes of the lamp by three points: a, b, and c.

ith point b, the coil is connected through the grid R1 C3 to the triode's grid, point a - directly to the cathode of this triode, and point c - to the ground, to which it is also connected through capacitance C4 and anode of the same triode.

At a certain position of the point a on the circuit coil, such a circuit generates its oscillations, i.e., the receiver turns into a generator. Stations should be received near the generation threshold, telegraph signals are received beyond the generation threshold when the receiver has just begun to generate, and telephone exchanges - before reaching the generation threshold, when the receiver is not yet generating. The closer to the generation threshold the station is received, the louder it is heard and the more stations the receiver can receive. Therefore, it is very important that the generation of the receiver, or, as they say, feedback, can be controlled.

The feedback adjustment in the receiver should be as smooth as possible. There are many different methods for adjusting the amount of feedback, but they are all more or less complex and difficult to set up. Our receiver uses a somewhat unusual method of adjusting the feedback. It is governed by variables! the resistance between the first triode's cathode and the ground. The resistance R2, connected to a part of the oscillatory circuit, introduces additional losses, increasing the circuit's attenuation.

By adjusting the value of this resistance, the receiver can be set to a mode corresponding to the generation threshold.

This circuit is simple and does not require a second variable capacitor for the receiver like other feedback adjustment circuits. As tests have shown, it gives a smooth approach to the generation threshold and detunes the receiver circuit to a lesser extent than when adjusting the feedback in circuits with a capacitor. The alternating voltage of the audio frequency is allocated to the anode load resistance R5, included in the anode circuit of the left triode. Through the capacitor Sv, this voltage is supplied to the second triode's grid, which operates as an audio frequency amplifier. The resistance R4 is the grid leakage.

To obtain a constant negative bias on the second triode's grid, resistance R5 is included in the cathode circuit, shunted by capacitor C5 to pass audio frequency currents. The anode load of this triode is telephones connected directly to the anode circuit. Phones are shunted by capacitor C7.

How To Make Receiver Parts

Make your receiver coils. They should be made in two pieces - for 40- and 20-meter amateur bands. Wind each coil on carbonite bases from old unusable lamps such as VO-188, UO-186, or others. The diameter of these bases is 38 mm. Clean the lamp's base from the remnants of glass and mastic, with which the bulb is glued to the base. For Coil #1 (for 40m bands), take 0.8mm enamelled wire and wind 19 turns tapped from the 7th turn, counting from the grounded end.

Pass the beginning and end of the coil inside the base through the holes that you pre-drill in the wall of the base. Next, pass both ends of the coil wire through the holes in the legs of the lamp base, peel off the insulation, and solder to these legs. If the wire does not go through the holes in the legs, then drill holes in the bottom of the plinth next to the legs.

Solder the beginning and end of the coil to the legs of the lamp base, as shown in fig. 3. Solder taps a to the coil, for which the wire at the soldering point must be stripped of insulation. To accurately select the position of the tap on the coil when adjusting the receiver, the wire should be stripped on two or three adjacent turns. Solder the tap to the anode leg of the lamp base, and pass the conductor from outside since it is somewhat difficult to pass it inside.

Simultaneously with training in listening reception, one should master the amateur "radio code," the tables for distributing call signs of amateur stations by country, and the rules for conducting amateur radio communications, etc.

Along with this, you need to take care of your shortwave receiver. The fact is that a conventional broadcast receiver is not suitable for receiving telegraph stations. On such a receiver (for example, on the receiver "Minsk," "Ural," "Rodina," "Record"), you can hear only a small number of amateur shortwave stations operating as a radiotelephone while receiving telegraph stations would require alteration of the receiver. It is much easier to build a dedicated shortwave receiver. First, you must choose the simplest circuit, so the receiver can easily build and set up. With this receiver, you can learn how to monitor the operation of shortwaves.

Receiver Circuit

The receiver's circuit is simple and has one twin lamp powered from the AC mains through a rectifier. The receiver operates on the 40- and 20-meter amateur bands and the transition from one band to another is done by changing the coil. The receiver works on a 6N9 M-type lamp. In the balloon of this lamp, there are two completely identical independent three-electrode lamps, which is why it is called a double triode. One lamp triode receives signals and detects them; the other is an audio frequency amplifier.

Thus, having only one lamp, our receiver is almost equivalent in volume to a two-tube receiver. The oscillatory circuit of the receiver consists of a self-induction coil L and a variable capacitor C2. The antenna is connected to the oscillatory circuit through the capacitor C1. This capacitor weakens the antenna's connection with the receiver's oscillatory circuit since, with a very strong connection (for example, when the antenna is connected directly to the circuit), the attenuation of the circuit increases, and the receiver stops working.

In addition, the capacitor C1 reduces the effect of the antenna capacitance on the receiver tuning; therefore, if the receiver is made exactly as described, then with any antenna, the amateur bands will not go out of the receiver scale. The winding of the coil should be carried out closely, coil to coil. When winding, the wire must be pulled as tightly as possible to prevent the coil from slipping.

Coil No. 2 (for the 20-meter range) is wound with a wire with a diameter of 1.0 mm, also in enamel insulation. It would help if you winded nine turns with a tap from the 3rd turn, counting from the grounded end. Solder all three leads to the legs in the same order as for coil No. 1. After winding coil No. 2, lay a thick thread between its turns, providing a gap between turns of 0.3-0.4 mm.

Install a conventional 5-pin lamp socket on the receiver chassis, including the sockets in the receiver circuitry. By inserting the coil into the socket, you include it in the circuit with all three ends. This design of interchangeable coils allows you to switch from one range to another quickly. This design also benefits a novice radio amateur by allowing you to manufacture and test one coil first and then start manufacturing another. In addition, it is possible to make coils for other amateur bands.

The tuning capacitor is made from any variable capacitor, in which two fixed plates with a distance of 7 mm between them and one movable one must be left. The remaining plates are removed. The maximum capacitance of such a capacitor will be 20-25 pF; the minimum is about ten pF. With such a capacitance of the capacitor, the amateur range is "stretched" by 15 - 20 degrees of the scale, and tuning to amateur stations can be done with a regular pen without a vernier. When overhauling the capacitor, carefully clean all contacts (especially rubbing ones) from dirt and oxide and adjust the rotor to rotate easily and smoothly.

You can also put a homemade capacitor in the receiver, making it from two plates: one movable and one fixed. The base of the capacitor is a plate made of organic glass, textiles, or ebonite. On this plate, fix the fixed plate of the condenser with two bolts and one telephone jack, which you place against the cutout of the fixed plate. Mount the moving plate on a single plug. Insert the plug firmly into the socket, so the distance between the capacitor plates is about 2 mm. Lengthen the plug handle by inserting an ebonite or wooden stick displayed on the receiver's front panel. Attach the capacitor with two screws to the horizontal panel of the chassis.

Capacitor plates are best made of brass or aluminum, 0.5 mm thick. Since the movable plate is connected to the circuit through a friction contact between the plug and the jack, strong crackling or noise can sometimes be heard in phones when the capacitor rotates. Connect the movable plate to the socket with a flexible copper conductor or ribbon to eliminate the harmful effect of rubbing contact. The antenna capacitor is of great importance for the normal operation of the receiver. Its capacitance should be small (5-10 pF). It is best to use a semi-variable capacitor for this purpose.

On a piece of 1.5 mm wire with enamel insulation, connected according to the scheme with the upper end of the coil, apply two layers of thin tissue paper and wind a turn to turn another wire with a diameter of 0.3-0.5 mm in double paper or silk insulation; winding length should be equal to 8-10 mm.
Connect a single end of this wire to the "antenna" terminal, and the other remains free. These two conductors, separated by insulation layers, form a

capacitor, the capacitance of which can be changed by unwinding or winding the turns of a thin wire.

All other receiver parts are factory; they must be purchased ready-made. Resistance R2 - variable, mastic. Its value can vary from 2-3 thousand to 10-15 thousand ohms. When purchasing this resistance, check its engine. It must have a smooth ride.

In any circuit, including our receiver, some parts require precise observance of electrical quantities. In contrast, others can be replaced with parts of suitable size without degrading the receiver's operation.

So, for example, in our receiver, the data of the following details can vary within: R1 = 1-2 mg, R3 = 1000-1500 ohm, R4 = 0.1-0.5 mg. C3 = 50-100 pF, C5 and C6 = 10-100 thousand pF, C4 = 500-1,000 pF, C7 = 1,000-5,000 pF.

It is best not to change the data of wires and turns of coils, the method of winding, and the frame's dimensions - this will facilitate the search for amateur stations when setting up the receiver. Otherwise, the receiver will be tuned to waves that are different from the amateur ones, and to find the desired bands, you will need to rewind the coils, which will take a lot of time.

In the described receiver, a lamp of the 5N9M type is used. The receiver was also tested on a 6N8M (6S N7) type lamp, which coincides with the pinout of the 6N9M lamp. On a 6H8M lamp, the receiver works without any changes in the circuit, but the results are somewhat worse. The best results are obtained with this lamp if the bias resistance R3 is reduced to 500 ohms. When switching to a 6H8M lamp, amateur ranges are slightly shifted to the side along the tuning scale.

Receiver Design

To mount the receiver parts, you need to make a chassis. For this purpose, it is best to take sheet aluminum with a 1-2 mm thickness. Make the vertical panel out of 2mm aluminum and the horizontal panel out of thinner aluminum (1mm). Fasten the horizontal panel with the vertical one with two or three bolts and nuts.

On the horizontal panel of the chassis are installed: a tuning capacitor, 8-pin lamp socket, socket for the coil on the vertical - variable resistance, antenna clamp, and telephone jacks. Through the front panel, bring out the tuning capacitor's axis, and put a handle (limb) with a 70-80 mm diameter on the axis. With such dimensions of the knob, even the weakest stations can be tuned (with a certain skill) without any special slowdown device. Chassis width 120mm.

The chassis can be made from copper, brass, or iron if aluminum is unavailable. A horizontal panel can be made of wood or plywood and pasted with a frame from a punched microfarad capacitor. At the end of the wooden plank, bend the frame and press it tightly under the vertical chassis panel. The vertical panel should be made of metal (aluminum or brass) since a wooden panel pasted over with steel does not shield the receiver from the influence of the operator's hands, and tuning the receiver becomes very difficult.

It would help to mount the receiver with a copper wire diameter of 0.8-1.5 mm. It is best to use a wire with insulation (no matter what). Connect the conductors by hot soldering with tin. Be especially careful when attaching a lamp socket to the circuit; the petal of the socket must correspond to the desired electrode.

Equipment Setup

You have built or purchased a transmitter or transceiver. The requirement to tune it to a ballast load is obvious and is known to everyone. However, one way or another, someday, you will need to match your transmitter with a specific antenna while the transmission of the tuning signal to the air is inevitable. To do this, it is desirable to choose the time in such a way that, at the moment, the passage on this range is minimal, i.e., this is, for example, daytime for the 80m band, nighttime, or close to it for the 10m band, etc. By the way, both of these recommendations are not the law because, for example, just before sunset on the 80 m band, the ultra-long passage can be observed, and at night in the 10 m band during the years of maximum solar activity, the passage can be very strong. The main thing is to listen to the frequency you will use before you turn on the transmitter. Remember: "Listen, listen, listen, and then listen some more.

Further, it should be your law that you should not tune your transmitter in the DX portion of the bands. And, of course, before you start tuning the transmitter, as we agreed, listen carefully to the frequency and ask if the frequency is busy ("Is the frequency in use?" in English and "QRL?" by telegraph). While tuning the transmitter, you must listen to your frequency occasionally: the transmission may change, and you may begin to interfere with other stations on recently free frequency. Having tuned the transmitter to a specific antenna, make marks next to the corresponding knobs so that you do not have to reconfigure the transmitter with each change from band to band.

To become a radio amateur, you must get an amateur radio license. Usually, it looks like this: you apply to the national amateur radio organization or directly to the communications administration of your country, pass a qualifying exam - yes, yes, you need to prove that you are sufficiently prepared to be entrusted with the right to use the radio station as a hobby (and not as a commercial user for money), and based on the passed exam you get a license and an assigned call sign. The call sign is the first and only name of the radio amateur by which he identifies himself and other radio amateurs; repeating, identical callsigns do not exist; all are unique.

Ham Radio Call signs

The structure of amateur callsigns is simple and logical but not without rare exceptions, which we will not focus on. A typical call sign looks like AB1CDE.

AB is a prefix by which a territory is uniquely identified (a country or a certain region of a country, if such a division is provided). It often consists of two letters, sometimes one letter, sometimes a letter, and a number. It is not difficult for those who are minimally interested in aviation to find that amateur radio prefixes are equal to ICAO prefixes.

1- one digit. This is a mandatory element of the amateur call sign, including distinguishing it from the aircraft's call sign. The number separates the callsign prefix from the suffix. However, suppose the prefix consists of a letter digit. In that case, the digit after the prefix is sometimes omitted, and only in exceptional cases (memorial call sign RAEM) is the digit not present. Most of the time, there is more than one digit, almost always a temporary call sign in honour of some event, some round date. In some countries, the number means nothing and is issued in order of increasing numbers or randomly. In some countries, the number indicates a specific geographic region. In some countries, the number means the license class or carries some other information.

CDE- a suffix consisting of one to four letters, usually prominent in order of increasing numbers. Sometimes the first or even the second letter can have a meaning, such as a geographic region of a country or a license class. There is no need to memorize all this; you need to understand the principles; frequently occurring call signs will be remembered by themselves, and unusual ones, obviously new to you, will cause an irresistible desire to "work" the station with a new call sign as soon as possible. Take, for example, the call sign W5UN - a real-life operator famous in his circles. W means the continental United States; there could be one letter or two, but this particular operator has one. 5 means a conditional region (AR, LA, MS, NM, OK, TX), and the letters Unreceived simply in turn or selected from those unoccupied. A conditional region is not guaranteed since, in the United States, it is allowed to keep your call sign when moving. It is also possible to receive a call sign of your choice (from free ones), including the digit of a foreign region. We can also assume from only four digits in the call sign, although this is a special case for the United States, that the operator has the highest license class, i.e., maximum tolerance. The fact is that in most countries (but not, say, in Japan) when you upgrade your license class, you are given the right to choose a shorter call sign. Still, not everyone uses this right, so a long call sign does not necessarily mean a low license class, but a short one almost always means a high-class license.

Let's take another example - P3X, also a real-life operator. By the prefix P3, we determine Cyprus; the number is generally omitted, and the suffix consists of only one letter X. This is a special callsign for competitions; it was issued to a radio amateur with a long everyday callsign 5B4AMM exclusively for use during radio sports competitions (we'll get back to the competitions), where 5B is the prefix, 4 is the digit separating the prefix, and AMM is the suffix of the callsign received in turn.

What Exactly Do Radio Amateurs Do?

The main directions are:

1. Design and manufacture of equipment and antennas. A modern radio station is a very complex device in design and manufacture, so the industry offers a variety of kits of varying degrees of complexity, making it possible for amateurs of different levels of training to assemble their radio and not leave it to individual engineers. Many owners of finished industrial radios solder simpler equipment simply because they like the process and not because they can't afford factory devices. The same goes for antennas and ancillary equipment, the manufacture of which for many is not a way to save money but a way to realize themselves in this hobby. But it's nice to establish a connection on your homemade product, even if it is inferior to the existing factory apparatus by orders of magnitude!

2. Sport. There are various radiosport competitions, the general principle of which is to make as many QSOs as possible in a fixed time, and conditional points value each QSO. The higher, the more technically difficult it is. There is no time for talking here, only to

correctly fix the very fact of establishing a connection - the exchange of call signs, reports on the strength of the received signal, and, as a rule, serial numbers, according to which the refereeing takes place. There are also various award programs in which the operator is not limited by time or the time frame is very wide - it is necessary to establish a certain number of QSOs according to the rules of a particular award program to receive a commemorative certificate or plate confirming the achievement. To fulfill the minimum conditions of the diploma, it is necessary to connect with at least one hundred "territories" on the DXCC list; today, there are 340. Usually, each administrative country is equal to one DXCC territory,

3. Just talk about radios and antennas and the like. Since the topic of radio is common to all radio amateurs, free talk somehow revolves around the radio. In some countries, negotiations are directly restricted - radio equipment and antennas, radio sports and radio wave propagation, and weather. Other countries have no explicit prohibitions, but the unwritten rule is still the same. Also, in some countries, there is an immediate ban on transmitting information from/to third parties, even if they are also radio amateurs. If you are not interested in such topics, you have nothing to do with radio amateurs because you will not find other topics for conversation. Politics, religion, commerce, and offensive behaviour are strictly prohibited. For everything that is not included in the subject allowed for radio amateurs, there is a CB band,

How Are Connections Made?

First, there are several types of signal modulation. Usually, they coincide, but it is possible to make connections in different forms. Communication is usually carried out simultaneously, but a small frequency spacing and even different ranges are often used. No one has their frequency. The currently unoccupied frequency is temporarily occupied by an operator making a general or directed call. Whoever hears him and wants to answer - answers. Then, when the calling operator finishes work or changes the frequency, the previously occupied frequency will be released, and anyone else can immediately take it. The calling operator first calls the call sign of the person he is calling or gives a general call, after which he calls his call sign. The operator answering him also first calls someone else's call sign - the one to whom he answers, and then his own.

Options For Signal Modulation

In terms of signal modulation, the following options are used. Telegraph, Morse code. Radio amateurs traditionally call it CW, while it would be more accurate to say A1A. Why did radio amateurs, who at the dawn of their inception were the vanguard of signalmen, who own many achievements in mastering the practice of radio communication, hit retrograde and still use an outdated type of modulation, which professional signallers have long abandoned, and in many countries the ability to transmit by hand and receive Is telegraph by ear still part of the qualifying exam? The point of view of the communications administrations of many countries would sound something like this: since amateur communications in emergency conditions can be used instead of commercial / state channels that have collapsed for some reason, it is necessary for operators to be able to communicate, including on home-made equipment from literally one transistor, because lives can depend on it.

But among the radio amateurs themselves, opinions differ. Someone claims that the telegraph is the most "long-range" type, which is not true ("digit" is "long-range"). Someone is far from technology and operates with concepts like "we taught - let them (beginners) also teach." And for adequate amateurs, the telegraph is just a sport because any sport has conditional restrictions called rules. Here radio athletes also like to play by such rules. The obvious difficulty of the telegraph is the need to master transmission (not very difficult) and reception (more difficult, but also not impossible). Also, the telegraph has a low data rate, but it is a great view for sporting purposes, despite the retrograde.

Types of Digital Telephony

Extensive section, with the vast majority owned by SSB (J3E). It should be noted that equipment designed for SSB is relatively difficult to design and configure, so the transition to SSB was resisted for a long time, remaining true to AM (A3E). But with the advent of commercial equipment and the publication of relatively affordable amateur developments, the transition to SSB successfully ended with an unconditional victory for SSB, which gives roughly half the occupied bandwidth with equal transmitted information, and this saves a scarce radio frequency resource, and the potential to improve the signal to noise ratio. Today, AM is practically not used. The second most popular by a disastrous margin is FM (F3E), which is much more common on amateur VHF bands or non-amateur CB bands. There are also various types of digital telephony when the operator's voice is digitized and transmitted as a data stream.

For now, these options can be considered rather experimental, although their role may significantly increase in the foreseeable future. Despite the seeming simplicity of making connections in telephony - which is even easier than taking a microphone and shouting, this is the most difficult method because it requires a greater signal-to-noise ratio than the telegraph and more than some types of "numbers." This means that the telephone operator needs better antennas to receive better the weak signals of his correspondents and to hear himself better. Also, the telephone operator should pay attention to the quality of his modulation - use high-quality microphones and channel strips to receive and pre-process the signal from the microphone unless such functionality is built directly into the radio.

After all, the better the signal is prepared, the easier it is to receive it at a low level, which means the more likely it is to conduct radio communication with someone hard to hear due to a long distance or weak equipment, and this, as luck would have it, is those territories with which communication is most Interesting. And at sufficiently high signal levels, when correspondents can hear subtle nuances, receiving compliments on your signal is nice. Telephony is generally near broadcasting and pro-audio, allowing enthusiasts to enjoy several hobbies simultaneously.

Letterpress Or "Number."

There is a huge number of completely different types of modulation here, the common thing for which is that the transmitter station uses a specialized device (in ~ 100% of cases, it is a general-purpose computer with a sound card, which emulates a specialized device), which receives a typewritten text from the keyboard, modulates it in a known way and sends it on the air. A similar device decodes the received signal on the receiving side and displays text on the screen. There are relatively high-speed modes that spit out quite a lot of information per unit of time, and there are relatively slow ones, which, due to the multiple redundancies of coding, make it possible to obtain stable reception of signals much weaker than an experienced telegrapher could accept.

Since most of the work is done by a computer and not by an operator, these are relatively simple types of communication that do not require a highly qualified operator or high-end equipment. Therefore they are attractive to beginners and to those who, for organizational reasons, cannot use the equipment better.

Chapter 3: Running Your Ham Radio Station

Let us briefly explain the radio station's operation principle (synonym - transceiver). Transceiver - translated from English, means a transceiver. (Transmit - transmit, Receive - receive, Transmitter - transceiver). As can be seen from the definition, the transceiver consists of two main parts: receiver and transmitter. The receiver and transmitter are complex devices assembled in one housing with common nodes. The task of the radio receiver is to convert the signal received from the radio frequency ether into a sound vibration perceived by the human ear. Modern radio signal receivers are built using a superheterodyne scheme (with double frequency conversion).

The receiver in a radio station starts with an antenna connector. The signal entering the connector is passed through a bandpass filter and amplified by a UHF high-frequency amplifier. Next, the signal is fed to the detector of the radio station, which extracts the low-frequency information component (for example, voice) from the signal. From the output of the detector, the signal enters the low-frequency amplifier (ULF), then the speaker. This converts the radio signal received through your radio's antenna connector into an audible audio signal.

Radio reception quality depends on the quality of all of the above nodes. That is why some radio stations receive loudly and clearly, and some with interference, mumbling, unintelligible. Also, the cause of the poor reception of the radio station may be errors in installing the antenna for the 27 MHz radio station. The quality of radio stations supplied to market is constantly changing; therefore, when choosing a radio station, we advise you to listen to the advice of specialists.

The Transmitter In A Radio Station

The task of the transmitter in the walkie-talkie is the opposite of the receiver: to broadcast information from one subscriber to another. In the transmitter of the radio station, a process is approximately the reverse of the process in the receiver: information (for radio stations, this is most often voice, although it can also be data) is superimposed on the carrier frequency set by the frequency generator and sent via cable, through the antenna on the air. Suppose we transmit information through a radio station using voice. In that case, the signal from the radio microphone is fed to the ULF (low-frequency amplifier) - the same node after the receiver, where it is amplified and fed to the modulator.

Modulator - a node in a radio station that changes the high-frequency (HF) radio signal sent on the air according to the law of changing the information signal (voice). In 27 MHz amateur radio, amplitude modulation (AM) and frequency modulation (FM or FM) are most commonly used. Amplitude modulation in a walkie-talkie is a change in the level of a high-frequency signal according to the law of voice change. In the final signal transmitted over the air, the signal's carrier frequency remains unchanged, but the amplitude changes. At the receiving end, the RF signal envelope is allocated; this envelope will be the information signal.

Frequency modulation in a radio station is a change in the frequency of the RF signal sent on the air according to the law of voice change. In this case, the RF signal has a constant amplitude, and the carrier frequency varies. At the receiving end of the FM, the detector selects the low-frequency signal and feeds it to the ULF and then to the speaker. There is also single-sideband SSB modulation (USB and LSB), which has more complex algorithms and is implemented in expensive devices. Therefore, it is not widely used in a 27 MHz radio station.

Step By Step Setting Of Ham Radio Transverter

It is recommended to start setting up any design by checking the correct installation. Tuning should begin with a quartz oscillator. It is necessary to connect the base of the 1T5 transistor to the case using a capacitor with a capacity of 1000-5000 pF. In this case, the quartz oscillator will turn into a conventional LC oscillator, the generation frequency of which is determined by the circuit 1L9 1C19 1C20.

By rotating the core of the 1L9 coil, it is necessary to set the generation frequency close to the triple frequency of the quartz resonator. After that, the blocking capacitor is disconnected from the base of the 1T5 transistor and fine-tuned to a position at which the rotation of the core of the IL9 coil has the least effect on the generation frequency.

In the presence of a receiver with a qualitative scale or, even better, an electronic counting frequency meter, the generation frequency should be checked and, if necessary, corrected. As is known, electrical correction methods are ineffective in circuits operating with the mechanical harmonics of a quartz resonator. Therefore, it remains only to change the parameters of the resonator itself. The situation is simplest if a quartz resonator with external metal plates is used, i.e., without metallization of the quartz plate. The frequency of such a resonator can be easily increased by 3-5% by grinding the plate on fine-grained sandpaper.

The frequency of such a resonator can be reduced to 0.5% of the nominal value by rubbing the central part of the plate with a piece of lead or solder. In this case, it should be considered that the plate treated in this way is subject to aging within 2-3 days. After that, the frequency change stops, and the quartz resonator works stably. It is much more difficult to correct the frequency of metalized quartz plates. If the plating is done with silver, the resonator's frequency can be increased by reducing the coating thickness using an ink eraser. For a more durable coating, you can use fine-grained abrasive paper.

Before turning on the quartz resonator in the circuit, it is necessary to wipe the plate with a cloth soaked in alcohol. Next, proceed to set up the chain of multipliers of the heterodyne path. When setting up the multipliers and all other stages of the transverter, it is necessary to control the operating modes of the transistors in direct current. It is most convenient to measure the voltage at the collector since, with a known resistance of the resistor in the collector circuit, it is easy to determine the current flowing through the transistor: I \u003d (Ep - Ek) / Rk, where I am the current flowing through the transistor. mA; Ep - power supply voltage, V; Ek - voltage on the collector of the transistor, V; Rk is the resistance of the collector resistor, kOhm.

A feature of the mode measurement is that this measurement must be carried out in working condition, that is, in the presence of a signal. The fact is that most of the transistors used in the radio station operate in large signal mode, which means that the operating modes for direct current and high frequency are interconnected. In this case, connecting the probe to the measuring device can affect the cascade's operation at high frequency and, thus, introduce an error in the measurements. Another danger is that even when measuring the mode of a transistor operating in the small signal mode, the cascade can be self-excited when the probe is connected.

Such self-excitation can significantly affect the operation of the transistor and thus distort the measurement results. To avoid such effects, it is required to make measurements through a resistor with a resistance of 10 kOhm or more. The resistor must be fixed at the probe's tip so that the conductor connected to the circuit has a minimum length. The presence of an additional resistor underestimates the voltmeter readings, but the resulting error is easy to consider. For the convenience of measurements, you can, for example, switch to a lower limit of the voltmeter. Then, having selected the resistance of an external resistor, return to the previous scale.

The establishment of the first triple, made on a 1T6 transistor, begins with adjusting the excitation mode. By selecting the capacitance of the 1C22 capacitor, it is necessary to ensure that the constant voltage on the collector of the transistor is 5-6 V. This corresponds to the collector current of the 1T6 transistor of about six mA. After that, they start setting up the dual-circuit filter 1L10 1C25-IL11 1C26. The setting is made according to the maximum collector current of the transistor /G7, which is in the next stage of the multiplier. The required degree of excitation of the 1T7 transistor can be adjusted by changing the connection point of the filter circuits to the collector of the IT6 transistor and the base of the 1T7 transistor.

Care must be taken when selecting taps on coils to load both circuits approximately equally. The value of the loaded quality factor of the circuit can be judged by the sharpness of the setting using a trimmer capacitor: If one of the circuits has a more "blunt" setting, then the tap on the coil should be soldered closer to the grounded terminal. With the correct setting, the constant voltage in the collector of the 1T7 transistor should be 5-6 V.

If the coil sizes 1L10 and 1L11 are sufficiently accurate, and the trimmer capacitors are approximately in the middle position, there is little danger of tuning the filter to the wrong harmonic. However, if the dimensions of the coils or the frequency of the crystal oscillator are changed, it is useful in one way or another to check the correctness of the setting. You can, for example, use a receiver operating in the desired frequency range. A piece of wire must be connected to the receiver's input, the other end of which should be brought to the 1L10 1C25 circuit. When rotating the tuning capacitor 1C25, the maximum volume of the signal must coincide with the maximum collector current of the transistor 1T7.

Testing Your Setup

The possibilities of this test method are limited by the fact that most communication receivers have an operating frequency range of no more than 25 MHz. You can expand the range of received frequencies using the simplest set-top box. The prefix is a quartz self-oscillator made on the GT311 transistor. At the same time, the transistor performs the functions of a mixer operating on the frequency harmonics of a quartz self-oscillator. To do this, the oscillator is connected to the input of a shortwave receiver using a piece of cable.

When establishing a heterodyne path, the prefix must be connected to the circuit of a tunable multiplier using a short piece of mounting wire. To do this, bring the insulated end of the mounting wire to the "hot" circuit output. There are no selective circuits in the prefix. That's why reception occurs simultaneously on many harmonics of the oscillator. It helps to understand the variety of signals that the frequencies of the local oscillator crystal oscillator and the set-top box crystal oscillator are known in advance. In the attachment, you can use any quartz resonator with a natural frequency of 8 to 15 MHz.

As an example, consider the process of tuning the 1L10 1C25 circuit to 61.5 MHz. Let the set-top box use a quartz resonator at a frequency of 9620 kHz, and check the transverter's crystal oscillator showed that its frequency is 20,504 kHz. Such a signal can be listened to using the fourth or fifth harmonic of the local oscillator of the set-top box. In the first case, the signal should be searched for at 61 512-9620-4=23 032 kHz. In the second case, which is suitable for receivers with a narrower operating range, the signal: must be sought at a frequency of 61512 - 9620*5 = 13412 kHz.

Expanding The Frequencies

It is possible to control the correct tuning of the multipliers up to 400-500 MHz frequencies. In principle, the frequency range can be expanded if a higher-frequency transistor is used and the capacitance of capacitors C2 and C4 is reduced. The correct setting of the multipliers can also be checked with a resonant wavemeter or, ideally, with a spectrum analyzer.

Let's continue consideration of a technique of adjustment of a local oscillator of a transverter 144/21 MHz. After the necessary excitation is applied to the base of the IT7 transistor, they begin to tune the 1L12 1C30 circuit to a frequency of 123 MHz. The cascade following the doubler is an amplifier based on a 1T8 transistor operating in class A mode. For this reason, the collector current of the IT8 transistor is weakly dependent on the excitation voltage and cannot serve to indicate the setting of the 1L12 1C30 doubler circuit.

Therefore, tuning must be done using a receiver or, in the simplest case, a high-frequency probe connected to the tester. The tester should be switched to the most sensitive DC measurement limit. The degree of connection of the probe with the circuit can be adjusted by moving the point of its connection to the coil or line.

After the 1L12 1C30 circuit is tuned to the desired frequency, they tune the terminal amplifier of the heterodyne path made on the 1T8 transistor. First of all, by selecting the resistance of the 1R20 resistor, it is necessary to set the collector current of the 1T8 transistor within 7-8 mA. The selection must be made in the absence of an excitation signal. After that, the 1T8 transistor must be excited and, using a high-frequency probe, set up the 1L13 1C34 circuit. This completes the local oscillator setup.

Setting Up The Receiving Path

Setting up the receiving path must begin with setting the modes of transistors 1T9 and 1T10 for direct current. By selecting resistors 1R22 and 1R26, the collector currents of the transistors should be set within 2-2.5 mA. After that, the mixer is connected to the input of a shortwave receiver tuned to a frequency of 21.2 MHz, and the circuit 1L18 1C50 1C51 1C52 is tuned to the maximum noise. After that, the high-frequency probe must be connected to the circuits 1L17 1C45, then to 1L16 1C43, and adjust the band-pass filter to the maximum of the local oscillator signal. Then, gradually reducing the capacitance of the trimmer capacitors, adjust the band-pass filter to the maximum noise. This adjustment procedure ensures that UHF is not tuned to the mirror channel.

The input circuit IL15 1C39 can only be configured with an input signal. Such a signal can, for example, be the fifth harmonic of a transmitter in the range of 28-29.7 MHz. To do this, shunt the converter's input with a 75-ohm resistor and connect a piece of wire 10-15 cm long as an antenna. You can also try to receive signals from two-meter radio stations. However, it is most convenient to use a noise signal source since, in this case, the tuning process is not affected by the instability of the frequency and level of the received signal. A 2D2S tube noise diode can be used as such a source. The key advantage of this source is that it generates noise of known power and can therefore be used to measure the noise figure of a receiver. The disadvantages include that the maximum noise intensity of such a source is low (20-50 kT0); moreover, the greater the noise intensity, the higher the cathode temperature and, consequently, the shorter the diode service life.

For this reason, it is better to save the noise diode for the final tuning of the receiver and use, for example, a semiconductor diode noise generator for preliminary tuning. The scheme of such a probe is shown in Fig. 27. The noise source is the emitter junction of the KT306 transistor operating in reverse voltage breakdown mode. In this case, the intensity of the generated noise is several hundred kT0. This makes it possible to improve the SWR of the probe by adding an attenuator on resistors R2 and R3 with an attenuation coefficient of 13 dB to its output. The probe is mounted in a small box with a cable to connect it to the receiver input.

During installation, special attention should be paid to the minimum length of the terminals of the transistor 77, resistors R2, R3, and capacitor C2. This is especially important if the probe is used to tune 432/21 and 1296/144 MHz transverters. The probe obtained a good result using a GA402 germanium microwave diode. The diode has a lower capacitance and lead inductance, which is especially important at high-frequency ranges. Adjusting the probe is reduced to setting the current through the diode 1-3 mA. For stable operation, the voltage of the power supply should be 2-3 times higher than the voltage at which the breakdown of the diode begins. The current is regulated by selecting the resistance of the resistor R1.

With this probe, you can easily tune the receive path to maximum gain. To do this, it is necessary to connect the tester to the output of the main receiver in the AC voltage measurement mode. Then, adjusting the circuits and selecting interstage connections achieves maximum readings. The final adjustment is made using a measuring noise generator. The technique for such adjustment will be described next.

Setting Up The Transmitting Path

Then you can proceed to set up the transmitting path. First, you need to set the transistor modes for direct current. By selecting the 1R10 resistor, the voltage on the collector of the 1T4 transistor is set to + 7 V, corresponding to a current of 10 mA. Using the 1R8 resistor, the 1T3 transistor mode is set. The voltage on the collector 1T3 should equal -И) V (collector current 20 mA). When adjusting the initial current of the terminal and terminal transistors, it is better to measure the DC voltage on the collector not relative to the ground but to the positive wire.

The voltage drop across the 1R4 resistor should be 4 V (100 mA), and the voltage drop across the IRt resistor should be 0.2 V (40 mA). After that, the supply voltage from transistors 1T1 and 1T2 must be temporarily turned off. Now you can start tuning the resonant circuits. The initial tuning is done without a signal with a frequency of 21 MHz. In this case, the resonant circuits 1L8 1C15, 1L7 1C14, and 1L6 1C10 are tuned to the local oscillator frequency, i.e., to 123 MHz. Tuning is carried out using a high-frequency probe connected to these circuits. Then, a signal with a frequency of 21.2 MHz must be applied to the mixer input.

The signal voltage must be increased until a noticeable decrease in the collector current of the 1T4 transistor begins. At the same time, circuit 1L14, 1C35, and 1C37 is adjusted. The local oscillator signal voltage at the mixer output should then decrease slightly. After that, the high-frequency probe must be loosely connected to the 1L8 resonator and, by rotating the 1C15 tuning capacitor in decreasing capacitance, find the nearest voltage maximum corresponding to a frequency of 144.2 MHz.

Now you can set up the last two stages of the transmitting path. Before that, to avoid failure of the transistor /G/, the output of the transmitting path must be connected to a load corresponding to the impedance of the feeder. Such a load can be made independently by connecting several parallel two-watt resistors of the MLT type. These can be, for example, four 300 ohm resistors if a feeder with a characteristic impedance of 75 ohms is to be used or six 300 ohm resistors if the feeder resistance is 50 ohms. The load resistors and the detector are placed in a small metal box with a high-frequency connector. Resistors R1-R4 are arranged in a star pattern relative to the connector and should have a minimum lead length. If the detector is provided with its dial indicator, then we will get a stand-alone device - the simplest power meter. In this case, it is desirable to introduce a switch that changes the resistance of the resistor R5 and hence the power measurement limit.

After the load is connected to the output of the transmitting path and the supply voltage is applied to the last two stages, they start setting up the 1LA 1C6 circuit. The setting is made according to the maximum collector current of the 1T1 transistor. Before this, transistor 171 must be connected to the load as much as possible, i.e., set the capacitor 1C1 to the maximum and the capacitor 1C2 to the minimum.

The collector current of the 1T1 transistor can reach 500 mA or more. If the excitation voltage is insufficient, it is useful to adjust all the preliminary stages again and slightly reduce the capacitances of the capacitors 1C5 and 1C7. The output circuit is adjusted to the maximum reading of the power indicator. The larger the capacitance of the capacitor 1C2, the weaker the connection with the load. With a weak connection and a maximum excitation level, the transistor can go into a high overvoltage mode, in which there is a danger that the transistor will go out of line. Therefore, such modes should be avoided.

Selection Of Best Equipment For Your Ham Radio Station

It is also important where we are going to install the station. It is not the same in the field, normally free from nearby interference, as in the city, with much more radioelectric contamination. Seeing the latest trends of an average radio amateur, we could say that we all want an inexpensive piece of equipment that covers most of our possibilities for doing radio. Hence, the boom that multimode (FM, CW, SSB) and multiband (HF, VHF, UHF) equipment is having. If what we want is to set up a station that allows us to " kill the bug " (do some DX on HF, use digital modes, keep QSOs with usual colleagues on 80 and 40 meters, use V and UHF repeaters, experiment with satellite contacts, connect with radio packet, APRS, etc.); Without a doubt, a good choice can be one of these teams.

Comparison Of Equipment From Different Brands

I have selected five teams to respond to what was previously said, belonging to three of the main brands of equipment manufacturers for radio amateurs, Kenwood, Yaesu, and ICOM. I must add that the nature of this comparison is purely didactic and free of any commercial interest toward any of the three brands.

Two of them, FT-847 and TS-2000, could be considered base equipment, and the other three, mobile or base-mobile.

We will first compare them according to the tests carried out by the ARRL. It must be taken into account that these measurements may have a certain margin of error due to the calibration of the respective measurement equipment and the adjustment of the transceivers themselves since it is almost impossible for all of them to be adjusted the same at the factory.

EQUIPMENT	TX	RX												
	Sp	IMD		MDS					BDR					
		3rd	5th	3.5	14	50	144	432	3.5			14		
									Twenty	5	Diff	Twenty	5	Diff
TS-2000	55	27	42	138	137	142	140	143	127	99	28	126	99	27
FT-847	50	28	51	137	136	140	142	141	109	82	27	109	82	27
IC-706	53	30	33	142	142	142	142	143	118	86	32	120	86	3. 4
FT-857	53	25	40	136	137	136	140	140	109	90	19	109	90	19
FT-897	53	23	37	137	137	142	140	139	111	85	26	109	85	26

In the first column on the left, we have the five selected teams; Three from Yaesu and the other two from Kenwood and Icom, respectively. Undoubtedly, Yaesu is the oldest in this type of equipment and currently has the most models in its catalogue. We differentiate the transmission measures from the reception ones in the first division.

In transmission, we have:

1. Sp.- It is the level of spuriousness in the transmitted signal. It refers to the cleanliness and purity of the signal; It is measured in dB, and the transmitter will be better the higher the value in the table.

2. IM D . - It is the intermodulation in the transmission of 3rd and 5th order produced by two close tones, for example, 1KHz and 2KHz, which are inserted into the modulator; It is measured in dB, and the transmitter will be better the higher the value in the table.

At the reception, we have:

1. MDS. is the minimum signal discernible by the receiver, also called sensitivity. It is measured in -dBm, and the receiver is more sensitive the higher the value in the table. It is an important piece of information if we want to capture weak signals, such as satellite reception.

2. BDR. - It is the dynamic blocking range, or capacity to eliminate the signals adjacent to the one we wish to receive, measured at 5 and 20 KHz, directly related to receptor selectivity. It is measured by placing the receiver on a frequency and putting next to another piece of equipment to transmit five or 20KHz higher, respectively. We begin by gradually increasing the power of the transmitting equipment until it interferes with the reception of the first signal.

3. IMDDR. - It is the dynamic range of the distortion by intermodulation, or quality of the receiver circuits of not generating false signals, in the presence of two strong signals at the input of the

receiver. It is measured in dB, and the receiver is better the higher the value in the table at 20 and 5KHz, and less the difference between them.

4. IP3 is the third-order intercept point many manufacturers give to highlight the receiver's quality. It results from a mathematical expression from the previous parameters. It is measured in dBm, and the receiver is better the higher its value.

At first glance, we can see that the TS-2000, unsurprisingly, offers the best values in almost all parameters. It is second only to a few in sensitivity by the IC-706MKIIG. This, in turn, outperforms all Yaesu in most parameters, even the FT-847. The differences between the FT-857 and FT-897, since both teams have the same internal electronics, the only thing that varies between them is practically the outer casing; hence what we mentioned at the beginning about the adjustment of the teams.

Now we go with a second comparison between these teams, related to the electronic components in their internal circuits. This table gives us an idea of the transistors used in the transmission line of the equipment.

Equipment	Power	Band	Final Transistor	Drivers	Driver	Amplifier	Preamplifier	Start
TS-2000	100	HF	2SC5125x2	2SC1972	2SC1971	2SK2596	2SK2596	
	100	VHF	2SC2694 x 2	x 2			uPC1678G	
	70	uhf	2SC3102	2SC3022	2SK2595	2SK2596		
FT-847	100	HF	2SC5125x2	MRF5015	MRF9745	uPC1677		
	fifty	VHF	2SC5125	PF0310	uPC1677			
	fifty	UHF	2SC3102	PF0340	uPC1677			
FT-897	100	HF	2SC5125x2	2SK2975	2SK2973 x 2	2SK2596	2SC3357	uPC2710
FT-857	50	VHF	2SC3102	x 2				
	20	UHF						
IC-706	100	HF	SRFJ7044 x 2	MRF1508	MXR9745 RT1	2SK2854	uPC2709	

Depending on your amateur radio experience, you can purchase more sophisticated equipment. But if you are a beginner, we suggest you start with simpler ham radio gear to put in the corner of the table and enjoy. And then set aside an entire room for your ham radio. To get started, purchase an amateur radio license. To become one of the radio amateurs, you need to know these things:

1. Security. Make sure the fire alarm system in your home is properly wired to use the ham radio;

2. Fixed antenna. They must be properly positioned and securely fastened;

3. Radios. It must work stably and be connected correctly.

4. Think carefully about how you set up and install your radios. Your enjoyment of your hobby depends on it.

Eliminate Radio Interference With Simple Means

In the home, radio interference is a major annoyance when stripes or blocks in the TV picture impair viewing pleasure, strange babble or whistling can be heard on the radio, or the reception is very poor. Such radio interference is often a source of conflict between a radio amateur and his neighbours. Both parties can be both affected and the causer. Enlightenment is needed in a language that even those who have never dealt with radio technology can understand. This article aims to help with that.

Fortunately, simple measures can remedy the situation in most cases without directly intervening in faulty or interfering devices. By the way, it's not just radios that can cause interference. The culprits are usually small plug-in power supplies, televisions, or computers that unreasonably interfere with the reception of amateurs, shortwave listeners, or FM radio without the polluter having the slightest idea about it. Some devices produce a steady hissing noise that makes all radio stations appear weak.

We look for a spot with no reception on an AM radio and turn the radio up loud. Then we turn on a lightbulb. The radio crackles. That's normal physics. A current pulse creates a multitude of radio waves of different frequencies. This is exactly what happens during a thunderstorm. We already have radio interference, which is so low with a light bulb that you can and must live with it. Remember this: Switching on creates a current pulse of many radio frequencies radiated via an antenna. In the case of the light bulb, the light network is the antenna.

The first radio transmitters were pop spark transmitters with the same principle. They could even be used to bridge the Atlantic. They were soon banned because they interfered with other radio services on a very broadband basis. Today it is mostly switching power supplies in which the desired voltages are generated with more than 30,000 switching operations per second. Due to the switch-on and switch-off times ratio, the voltage can be kept constant very effectively, and heavy and expensive transformers are no longer required for the 50 Hz AC voltage. In addition, the power loss is relatively low. Unfortunately, these switching processes can radiate a lot of high frequency into the power lines and other supply lines if countermeasures are not taken regarding circuitry, some of which cost money. That's why there are well-designed devices that cause little or no disruption, and there are products that cause a lot of disruption. A small plug-in power supply can then be 100 times more disruptive than the large TV in the living room.

Type Of Interference

There can be the following problems between a radio amateur and his neighbours, which can be remedied in most cases with very simple means:

1st case: The radio amateur feels considerably disturbed by the interference from electronic devices in the vicinity. It can no longer receive weak stations because they are lost in the noise and crackle of the interference emissions. The causes are usually poorly designed televisions, radios, power packs, computers, and many other electronic devices, which emit high frequencies into the antenna and the light network and thus impair reception within a radius of up to several 100 meters. Recently there have been increasing reports of disruptive inverters in solar systems. The inverters convert the DC voltage from the solar cells into the AC voltage of the power grid.

The radio amateur pays fees yearly to use his frequencies and asks the Federal Network Agency for help. In this case, the Federal Network Agency is entitled to work in private homes if an appointment is made. If a person refuses, this can be enforced with violence in extreme cases. So if the Federal Network Agency rings at the apartment door, it's no use not opening it. They come back, if necessary, accompanied by the police. And then it gets expensive.

So if the radio amateur notices that his neighbours are unwilling to cooperate in eliminating the interference, he will call the Federal Network Agency with his expertise sooner or later. As a rule, they will use a measuring vehicle to get to the bottom of the cause.

2nd case: The radio amateur seems to be interfering. Common disturbances are picture disturbances that occur periodically at irregular intervals of seconds to minutes, babbling from the loudspeaker or the telephone handset. Contact the radio amateur and describe the type of interference and when it occurs. It is part of his training to recognize and rectify such faults. He will be most interested in getting to the bottom of the causes and eliminating them. To do this, he needs your help. Could you not ask him to stop his hobby? Amateur radio is more than just a hobby for many radio amateurs. For them, belonging to a large international community is a special attitude toward life.

Remedy: Interestingly, the technical solution in both cases is the same in most cases. On the one hand, the interference immunity of the disturbed devices must be improved. On the other hand, the undesired high-frequency emissions from the interfering devices must be prevented. In both cases, the high-frequency flows into the disturbed devices via the supply lines, or, in the opposite case, the interfering high-frequency is radiated via the supply lines. The mains cables, speaker cables, audio cables, antenna cables, telephone cables, and so on are questioned. These cables act like transmitting or receiving antennas. Filters are installed in the lines to suppress interference to ensure no radiation or radiation through these lines. What is good soundproofing in residential construction is good high-frequency decoupling in electronics. Disturbances caused by direct radiation – i.e., not via cables – are rare.

Finding a Ham Radio Club

Ham radio clubs have existed since the inception of ham radio, offering a convenient avenue for communicating with other enthusiasts. During the early stages, these clubs were composed of individuals who shared common interests and worked together to build radios when the technology was still in its infancy, and success was not guaranteed.

Ham radio clubs are excellent sources of support and guidance for those just starting. As a newcomer to ham radio, you're bound to have numerous basic questions that require answers. It's a good idea to join a ham radio club that caters to general interests and, if possible, prioritizes providing support to new enthusiasts. Being in the company of like-minded individuals can make the journey to enjoying ham radio much smoother.

Many ham radio operators belong to one or more clubs, including a general interest club and one or two specialized interest clubs. Local or regional clubs usually hold physical meetings and draw members from a specific geographic area. In contrast, specialized clubs focus on particular activities, such as contesting, low-power operation, or amateur television, and may have members spread across various locations. Some club branches conduct their meetings exclusively via radio transmissions instead of face-to-face gatherings.

A simple online search can be conducted to locate local ham radio clubs, or the American Radio Relay League (ARRL) website can be consulted for a directory of affiliated clubs based on location. General interest clubs that offer assistance to new hams should be prioritized.

If multiple ham radio clubs exist in the area, meeting times should be compared, and the most convenient option should be selected. For those with specific interests, it is advisable to investigate whether local clubs devote time to them. Attending several meetings at different clubs can help identify the best fit.

In general, the challenge is not in finding a ham radio club but in selecting the most suitable one. Unless the club emphasizes personal participation, such as public service clubs, one can join as many clubs as desired to explore specific aspects of ham radio. Most clubs provide newsletters and websites that offer insight into their unique specialties.

After joining a general interest ham radio club, active participation is encouraged by attending meetings, making new acquaintances, and volunteering to assist with preparations and cleanup. The level of benefit derived from the club is commensurate with the level of involvement.

How To Promote Your Channel?

Feedback on the Internet implies new opportunities: user control over the content of the site, participation in the formation of content through posing problems for coverage and discussion, proactive position in the discussion of the resource, its authorship, exchange of views on various issues with a journalist and other users. New communication models are emerging thanks to this process, and alternative data collection and analysis methods are emerging.

The situation is unstable in the modern FM band and changes yearly, so the radio station is forced to look for new ways to survive in the modern media market. It is necessary to use new ways to promote your product, and for this, there is little airtime, so radio stations continue their activities. They communicate with their audience also off the air. To be successful today, a radio station needs to maintain its image and improve its content in three ways:

1. As a media outlet

2. As a commercial enterprise and an effective advertising medium

3. As an enterprise acting in the interests of the audience

And in all these areas, it is necessary to receive feedback from the audience, analyze the market and understand what kind of listener the radio station is targeting and what part of the audience needs to be attracted for further growth. Based on this, we can single out the main ways of off-air communication with the audience and promotion of the radio station:

1. Advertising

2. Public relations

3. Promo campaigns

4. Holding public events

5. Use of Internet marketing opportunities.

Selecting The Antenna For Radio Station

When you buy or build an antenna, you expect it to work efficiently and its signal will outperform other antennas. Will it be the right antenna for what you expect from it? The Nobel radio amateur knows that the function of an antenna is to emit and receive an electromagnetic signal that propagates through space. Still, he does not know how this prodigy of physics occurs. Before starting with the subject, I must inform you that there are no miraculous antennas, neither good, nor bad, nor worse; they all do the job they have been entrusted to; when it does not meet expectations, it could be that there is a bad choice or wrong mathematical calculations.

The radio station regardless of whether it is commercial or amateur radio, to be efficient, the technician, in this case, your amateur radio, has to know how to make the corresponding calculations to balance the impedance of the antenna, the appropriate height of the tower, and the length of the transmission line (coaxial cable); all this to deliver to space all the power delivered by the transmitter, taking advantage of the gain of the antenna.

Radio equipment is a branch of " electronics, particularly the branch of radio waves (wireless communication). More specifically, the technology of conducting radio broadcasting is the equipment used to transmit and receive radio waves: the radio transmitter, the transmission line, and the antennas. Still, the antennas are in charge of making the wonder of wireless communications by emitting and receiving waves. The dipole is undoubtedly one of the HF antennas that head the ladder (the level classification) of preferences due to its cost/performance ratio. Although it is the first antenna that an amateur radio plans to install to operate in HF when putting the theory into practice, some interesting details appear to be commented on.

For an amateur radio station to be efficient, its owner must apply his minimum theoretical knowledge of radio techniques to practice:

1. Technical conditions (regarding size.

2. Height above ground level.

3. Polarization

4. Standing Wave Ratio (SWR)

5. Type of soil

Separation concerning other antennas or constructive elements necessary for the operation of the antennas. Antennas for HF bands. Due to what is specified in the background, we will refer to the HF antennas (3-30 MHz), which are the ones that require the greatest space and height. As a starting point, it must be pointed out that the size of the antenna is directly proportional to the wavelength (l) corresponding to the frequency band in which it has to serve its function, making it impossible to reduce its size without losing its efficiency.

Considerations: Altitude + height.

Appropriate height of the antenna with the operating frequency. An antenna will be more effective the higher its height above the ground and sea level and the clearer it is of obstacles around it. The altitude above sea level of an antenna is something that radio amateurs cannot choose because each one will have to put it where they live. On the other hand, they can act on the height of the ground, raising it as much as possible above the ground. Using masts or towers. It is best to place the antenna as high as possible, especially for frequencies from 14 MHz onwards. The desirable height is between the half wavelength and the full wave. For example, in 14 MHz or a 20-meter band, the ideal minimum height will be 10 meters and the maximum 20, so we can conclude that the heights between 10, 5, and 21 meters are sufficient for all bands, although higher heights are achieved so much the better. However, the minimum height recommended by the American Radio Relay League (ARRL) antenna manual can be considered.

Chapter 4: Ham Radio Jargon

Suppose the QSO takes place between stations of different countries. In that case, we can point out that in such circumstances, a "radio amateur's lingua franca" is spoken, that is, a simplified variant of English to which the vocabulary of radio amateurs is added; if the connection, on the other hand, takes place between operators who belong to the same linguistic community, we obviously cannot speak of a "lingua franca." So we try to get away with some reference to "amateur radio jargon" or an "amateur radio specialist language," etc.

In short, since, at times, the answers are not adequately argued, it seems that a moment of reflection on the matter is necessary, perhaps taking a cue from the observation that people who have some interest in common, as it happens, precisely, to radio amateurs, tend to aggregate into groups whose members communicate with each other using a language that is difficult for outsiders to understand.

Linguists speak of "jargon" when the language used, which can also include visual or non-verbal phonic signs, has cryptic aspects specially developed to make the messages incomprehensible to outside the group (for example, youth jargons, school jargons underworld, etc.); on the other hand, we speak of a "specialist language" (1) when the difficulty of understanding by strangers is exclusively due to the presence, in the verbal messages, of some recurring morphological structures and a specific lexicon which is not present in the same forms, in the standard language (as, for example, in the idioms of professions, trades, etc.).

Since in amateur radio communications, there can be no search for secrecy as "the amateur radio activity consists in carrying out a service, carried out in clear language, or with the use of internationally accepted codes..."(2), it is it it is clear that the expression "amateur radio jargon" is not appropriate while the presence of a particular lexicon, mainly made up of the internationally accepted codes mentioned above, helps to give the messages exchanged in the QSOs the characteristics that generally belong to specialized languages. The internationally accepted codes that characterize the specialist amateur radio language are mostly presented as short forms, i.e., symbols, abbreviations, acronyms, and code words. We will briefly examine the meaning of these short forms in the current language below before dealing in more detail with the influence that each of them can have on the language spoken by radio amateurs.

The Different Types Of Short Forms

In particular, when the conciseness and immediacy of linguistic communication seem to prioritize completeness and clarity, single words or entire sentences are replaced by short forms that can be communicated more easily and faster, which we will illustrate the main characteristics in the list below.

The symbol represents something else: for example, the letter S is the chemical symbol of sulphur, the graphic sign [θ], in phonetic transcription, represents the initial sound of the English word thing, the scales are the symbol of justice, etc. The abbreviation consists of using a part of the word instead of the whole form as, for example, tel., prof., pag., etc.

The acronym is formed by the initial letter or letters of the name of companies, bodies, associations, parties, people, or denominations of any kind; the set of letters does not necessarily have to give rise to a new word with a full meaning. For example, LCD stands for Liquid Crystal Display, and BTPs are Long-Term Treasuries. The acronym (3), considered by many to be a synonym of the acronym (Devoto-Oli), for others, has the peculiar characteristic of being formed in a similar way to the acronym but to obtain a new word with complete meaning or that at least can be pronounced without spelling out the individual letters, such as LUCE for the Educational Cinematographic Union or FIAT for Fabbrica Italiana Automobili Torino or BASIC for Beginner's All-purpose Symbolic Instruction Code, etc. Due to this characteristic, acronyms probably succeed, more frequently than acronyms, in supplanting the original extended forms and entering the vocabulary as new words.

The code has, among many other meanings, also that of a set of alphabetic, numerical, or other signs and rules that allow the interpretation of their meaning. In daily use, there is a certain alternation between the terms listed above, which does not create problems worthy of note unless the context requires particular lexical precision, as in the case of the "callsign" of radio amateurs, of which we will deal with the short forms used in amateur radio activity.

The Short Forms In Amateur Radio Communications

All amateur radio communications are affected by the habits of using telegraphy. Radio amateurs who, by choice or for other reasons, are not interested in CW transmissions regularly use the lexicon developed by radio operators. Since the Morse code requires the transmission of several signs for every single letter to be communicated - short signals, long signals, and pauses of different lengths - it is easy to understand the propensity of telegraphers to use short forms in place of whole words (for ex . : TNX for THANKS, PSE for PLEASE, U for YOU, etc.), and also to the adoption of a special code, called Q code, with which, by sending a few letters, even quite complex information can be requested or sent.

On the other hand, also commercial telegraphy has accustomed users, due to the high costs, to use a short style whose denomination, entered the current language, is, in fact, that of "telegraphic style. " With the diffusion of voice transmissions, the "telegraphic style" would no longer have been strictly necessary. Still, the specialized amateur radio language, now consolidated, continued to use most of the short forms adopted by radio operators.

The first short form to take into consideration, speaking of radio amateurs, is undoubtedly the univocal callsign which is assigned to each operator, and which is not an abbreviation because taken as a whole, it does not abbreviate anything, it is not an acronym, because the letters and numbers that compose it are not necessarily the initials of other words and, even more so, it is not an acronym. It should rather be understood as a synthetic message, expressed in a specially created code, which allows identifying, with a combination of letters and numbers, the individual amateur radio, the country, and the area from which it transmits, and, in some cases, also the type of activities that it is authorized to carry out. Among the very numerous short forms that form the nucleus of the lexicon of the specialist amateur radio language, the ones listed below should at least be mentioned:

1. The SYMBOLS of mathematics, physics, electrical engineering, electronics, and radio engineering, which, however, for the most part, are not communicated briefly in voice transmissions.

2. Abbreviations, especially used in telegraphic communications and digital modes. The ABBREVIATIONS and abbreviations found on the control panels of transceivers, amplifiers, tuners, etc., and often mentioned in QSOs.

3. SYMBOLS, ACRONYMS, Or ACRONYMS used in the manuals of amateur radio equipment.

4. The Q CODE, already mentioned, was created to shorten, and facilitate telegraphic communications but remained used in telephone communications.

Naturally, any attempt to deal with the numerous short forms entered the specialized amateur radio language would require adequate specific skills and be unrealistic in this context. However, we can limit ourselves to proposing a few examples that allow us to highlight the pronunciation problems that can arise when the corresponding short forms are used instead of the extended forms.

The Pronunciation Of Amateur Radio Short Forms

The correct pronunciation of the short forms, even more than that of the English language words from which they mostly derive, can create some non-negligible difficulties for non-English-speaking operators. We will provide some examples below.

1. The PTT, the button to press into the transmission, is an excellent example of an acronym that has taken on an independent existence concerning the original PUSH TO TALK (PRESS TO TALK). If one takes into account the initial expression when a manual reads "press the PTT and speak into the microphone," it should mean "press the push to speak and speak into the microphone" (sic!).

2. S METER stands for SIGNAL METER and is the instrument that measures, among other things, the intensity of the signal. Some amateur radio, influenced by the widespread use in the citizen band, transforms it into SMITTER.

3. LSB and USB are abbreviations from LOWER SIDE BAND and UPPER SIDE BAND. A further complication is added by the presence, on many devices, of one or more USB sockets from the UNIVERSAL SERIAL BUS.

4. The acronym SWR is not so frequently used in QSOs, perhaps due to the difficult pronunciation while the corresponding Italian acronym ROS is widely used. Often, however, the expressions from which the two short forms derive are used, namely STANDING WAVE RATIO and STATIONARY WAVE RATIO

5. The abbreviation DSP, from DIGITAL SIGNAL PROCESSING has appeared in amateur radio conversations since many transceivers allow digital processing of the audio signal. The extended form is rarely used, and the acronym is pronounced, depending on the circumstances

Perhaps these few examples are enough to demonstrate that the pronunciation of the short forms most frequently used in QSOs deserves more attention than the one it receives in many cases.

Speaking Is Short, But Only For Other Radio Amateurs

Just as belonging to a national community is enhanced by using a shared language, the awareness of belonging to a group whose members cultivate the same interests is certainly strengthened by the possibility of expressing oneself through specialized jargon or language.

The same goes for radio amateurs who, especially in voice transmissions, could easily do without most of the short forms they use in QSOs but who, in doing so, would give up the most significant trait which certifies their belonging to the world community of to which they belong.

Just as happens, for example, in the medical field, where there are important differences between the variants of the specialized language spoken by technicians, nurses, general practitioners, or specialists, also in amateur radio communications, the messages present levels of complexity which vary with the variation of the technical and linguistic skills of the operators.

However, even when it seems that the only language used is the current one, the specialized lexicon and the related short forms frequently re-emerge in amateur radio transmissions, which, ultimately, are so strongly influenced by the "internationally accepted codes" that other radio amateurs can fully understand them.

Chapter 5: The FCC Exam System

Is FCC license necessary for my two-way radio use in the United States? The two types of radios are GMRS and FRS. The FCC mandates that any two-way radio in the United States that uses GMRS frequencies must obtain an FCC license. GMRS radios utilize channels around 462 MHz and 467 MHz and are commonly used for short-term communication through handheld radios, mobile radios, and repeaters. On the other hand, FRS (Family Radio Service) radios, also known as Walkie-Talkies, are frequently used by consumers and families and do not require an FCC license to operate.

Why is an FCC license required? The FCC is responsible for regulating the frequencies utilized in two-way radios. Possessing an FCC license allows you to operate on your frequencies, decreasing the risk of interfering with other channels. If you operate a business that employs portable two-way radios for communication but lacks an FCC license, the FCC is unaware of your use of those frequencies. Consequently, at any moment, those frequencies could be assigned to someone else, depriving you of communication and potentially resulting in a fine from the FCC. A license ensures that your frequencies do not conflict with anyone else's, and the small license fee is far preferable to the complaints and fines that may.

The Process For Obtaining An FCC License

If you know that your radio requires an FCC license, the next step is to apply for one. The application process is straightforward. The processing time for a typical business and industrial license is approximately ten business days, while a public safety license takes about 90-120 days. First, you must obtain an FRN (FCC Registration Number) from the FCC.GOV website. The quickest method to receive your FRN is to register online. After receiving your FRN, log in to your account, choose "Request a new license" from the top right corner, and follow the on-screen instructions.

The FCC necessitates the completion of Forms 159 and 605, which can be found on your application page. When applying for your license, you must provide your business name, address, and Federal Tax ID (if applicable). Additionally, you must inform them how many GMRS radios you own or intend to buy for the license. It is not necessary to have an FCC license before purchasing GMRS radios. After applying, it takes around ten business days to process, and you can locate it by using the ULS Application Search and entering the file number. On the following business day, double-check that your application was submitted accurately by clicking the "Search for applications" button in your account.

What Is The Cost Of An FCC License?

The FCC license fee is $70.00 and is valid for ten years. Some government entities are exempt from paying this fee. The license can be renewed 90 days before it expires. If your license expires, you must submit a new application.

FCC Licensing Checklist

Use this checklist to be sure that you have completed all task needed
1. Obtain an FRN number

2. Click "Apply for a new license" in your account

3. Fill out form 159 – Remittance Advice

4. Fill out form 605 – General Mobile Radio Services

5. Check on application status the following business day

What Equipment Is Subject To FCC Certification?

Unintentional radiation emitters, in the context of engineering, refer to electrical or electronic equipment that produces radio frequency energy for its use or transmits conducted radio frequency signals to associated equipment via a wired connection without intentionally emitting RF energy through radiation or induction. This description includes most electrical and electronic devices without wireless connectivity, such as coffee machines, cash registers, printers, non-cordless phones, and thousands of other commonly used digital technology equipment. Also included are those traditional products that at the time were considered emitters of accidental radiation, such as motors or power tools that now use digital logic. On the other hand, intentional radiation emitters are equipment whose design implements or generates radio frequency wirelessly; this classification includes mobile phones, short-range devices, IoT sensors, and remote-control equipment.

FCC Title 47 Part 15 groups RF devices into broad categories based on their operability:

1. Unintentional Radiators (Part 15B)

2. Intentional Radiators (Part 15C)

3. Non-Band Personal Communication Devices (Part 15D)

4. Devices of the national information infrastructure by the unlicensed band (Part 15E)

5. Ultra-Wideband Operation (Part 15F)

6. Broadband access by electricity network (Part 15G)

7. White Space Devices (Part 15F)

Other equipment covered by FCC certification under Title 47 are:

1. Cellular telephones and devices for the public mobile network (Part 22)

2. Personal Communication Services (Part 24)

3. Satellite communication equipment (Part 25), such as radio equipment, requires a license.

The scope of FCC certification separates equipment depending on how it uses the radio band, between licensed bands that require prior authorization and free bands, also known as unlicensed bands. Unlicensed band RF equipment is covered by FCC Rules, Parts 15 and 18. Part 15B and Part 18, relating to 'Unintentional Radiators' and 'Industrial, Scientific and Medical Equipment' respectively, are subject to voluntary certification, both unintentional radiators.

FCC Certification Step by Step

Before commencing the certification process for marketing radio equipment in the United States, an applicant must acquire an FCC Registration Number (FRN). This ten-digit number serves the purpose of identifying an individual or organization that has an association with the FCC. Once the FRN is obtained, the applicant must apply for a Grantee Code from the Commission via the Grantee Registration website. The Grantee Code is necessary for the first certification application and can be utilized for all subsequent certifications. After completing these steps, the applicant can begin the certification process with an FCC-recognized certification body.

There are different certification programs, depending on the nature of the telecommunications equipment. There are different ways to obtain approval depending on the applicant's needs, including Original Certification, FCC ID Change, or Modification (C2PC, C3PC). For each type of request, the requestor must provide a sample of the equipment to be tested in an FCC-authorized laboratory

Three Types Of Exams

The Federal Communications Commission (FCC) has three distinct approval processes: verification, declaration of conformity, and certification. Depending on the product and processes involved, obtaining FCC certification approval is the responsibility of either the FCC or a Telecommunications Certification Body (TCB). These authorized institutions are responsible for ensuring that the product meets the requirements for approval. Generally, electronic devices that require FCC certification must first undergo testing in a certified testing lab. The TCB will then evaluate the device's test reports and technical documentation to determine if it meets the required standards. The TCB will initiate the necessary administrative procedures for certification approval if the product is deemed suitable. If a manufacturer of electronic equipment wanted to expand its US market, it should obtain FCC certification.

Requirements For The Amateur Radio License USA

You can't be a member of the government. Otherwise, no requirements, e.g., age, health, nationality, or place of residence. However, a valid US address is required to deliver the FCC (American Telecommunications Authority/Federal Communication Commission) certificate. Since this is not sent abroad, anyone without acquaintances or relatives in the USA can rent a PO box. Registration with the FCC is mandatory; you will receive a so-called FRN (Federal Registration Number) to later register in the system. Choosing a desired call sign (vanity call sign) later is much easier with this number.

You need to be able to do the following to take the test

1. At least two government-issued IDs, one of which has a photo (ID, passport, driver's license, etc.)

2. A valid US mailing address can also be c/o a friend's address. Rental mailboxes or rental addresses are also possible.

3. For advancement exams (upgrade, e.g., from Technician Class to General Class): FCC license certificate or CSCE (original + copy)

4. US citizens need their social security number (SSN) or a tax identification number (TIN)

5. Pencils, erasers, ballpoint pens, Calculator (non-programmable)

6. The license application must be filled out at the beginning of the exam.

The Examination Procedure for The Amateur Radio License USA

The exam questions are organized based on the multiple-choice format and presented in English, while the exam will be conducted in English. The license exams are designed with a hierarchical structure, where passing each exam is a prerequisite for the next license level. It is possible to take all three exams at once.

1. The Technician Class license requires a 35-question multiple-choice exam with a passing score of 26.

2. The General Class license requires passing the Technician exam and a 35-question multiple-choice exam with a passing score of 26.

3. The Amateur Extra Class license requires passing the same exams as the General, along with a 50-question multiple-choice theory test, where a passing score is 38 or more. Licenses are valid for ten years from the date of issuance or renewal and can be renewed online for free.

Structure of FCC exams

The written exam is divided into sections, each with its passing criteria. The first section, Element 1, requires a passing score of 18 out of 24 questions and covers basic radio laws and operating practices. Element 3 assesses general radiotelephone knowledge, with the examinee needing to answer 75 out of 100 questions correctly in various categories. Technical, legal, and operational matters for all radiotelegraph stations are covered in Element 6, with a passing score of 75 out of 100. For Element 7, the examinee must correctly answer 75 out of 100 questions on GMDSS radio operating practices across different categories. Element 7R is specifically for restricted GMDSS radio operating practices, requiring at least 38 out of 50 questions to be answered correctly. Ship radar techniques are covered in Element 8, with a passing score of at least 38 out of 50 questions. Finally, Element 9 assesses GMDSS radio maintenance practices and procedures, requiring at least 38 out of 50 questions to be answered correctly.

The Telegraphy Examination is comprised of two required elements. The first element involves copying 16 code groups per minute, while the second requires copying 20 words per minute. The examination may include sending and receiving tests, and the examinee must send and receive the required speeds for one minute without making any mistakes. The code groups must be sent and received by ear in international Morse code, using letters, numbers, and punctuation marks, with each punctuation mark and number counting as two letters. The examination lasts approximately five minutes for each test, and if the examinee fails any part of the test, the examination will automatically end. The code speeds are calculated using five letters per word or code group.

Chapter 6: Technician FCC Exam Guide & Examples

Useful Tips for the Ham Radio Exam

First, most newcomers opt to prepare for and take the FCC's Technician class exam, the entry-level license that gives you the chance to get on the air quickly. Even if you intend to pursue the General or the highest level Amateur Extra class license, you must first obtain the Technician class license. Therefore, the Tech license serves as your starting point. If you plan on taking the General and even the Extra exam all in one go, you can save money on exam fees for the additional tests by taking them simultaneously. This is one advantage to consider. However, it is recommended that you start by studying for the Technician exam, and if you feel confident, you can contemplate pursuing one or two more classes of licenses.

1. Today's world has migrated that process online. Multiple online websites will help you understand the basic structure and practice tests for preparation.

2. It is important to allocate sufficient study time to obtain your ham license. Setting aside a fixed daily or weekly schedule allows you to focus on learning. For instance, you could set aside 30 minutes each day, perhaps after dinner, to review the study material or attempt the simulated online exam.

3. Sticking to your schedule will make you feel more comfortable with the study material and prepare you to take your first amateur radio license test in no time.

4. Adhering to your established schedule is crucial to the success of your studying. If you take a break for several weeks during your studies, you may forget some of the material. However, if you keep challenging yourself by studying every day or week and taking simulated tests, you will be better prepared in a shorter amount of time without the need to re-study because of time off.

5. Additionally, setting a test date goal can help you establish a timeframe for obtaining your ham radio license.

First, you should locate a list of amateur radio exam test sessions in your area. This is why it is essential to pace yourself. After deciding on the date for your exam, which could be weeks or months in advance depending on your local schedule and how much time you need to study, you can work backward and determine the amount of time you need to dedicate on a daily or weekly basis to be fully prepared on test day. Although it's unnecessary, some individuals pursuing their ham licenses desire to learn all aspects of the information, regulations, theory, science, and more, even if they don't require it to pass the FCC test. This is not necessarily a negative thing. Most study resources focus on comprehending the answers to pass the test.

The FCC ham radio exams use authorized question pools administered by radio clubs, so you know exactly what to study. Study all the questions, remember the correct answers, and you'll get your ham license! The question pools are available to the public, with questions, answer options, and correct responses. It's not complicated; if you have a good memory, you might even memorize all the correct answers.

Sample Test for FCC Technician Exam

Here we will discuss some sample questions and their correct answers to give an overview of the exam. These are some typical questions that are frequently asked during exams. Besides this, you can also practice for these tests online on multiple websites, showing you your score at the end of the test so you can figure out your weak areas.

Question 1. How can amateur radio operators utilize their transmissions to aid in broadcasting, program creation, or news gathering when alternative communication methods are unavailable?

Option A: When amateur radio operators gather and supply non-commercial programming solely to the National Public Radio network.

Option B: Never

Option C: In situations where amateur radio transmissions are used for property protection.

Option D: When using amateur radio to transmit communication to the space shuttle.

Option C specifies that amateur stations can only transmit safety or property protection information when supporting broadcasting, program production, or news gathering. The FCC prohibits amateur radio transmissions for commercial or entertainment-related purposes and regulates amateur radio operations in the US. Amateur radio operators are authorized to transmit on specific frequencies and may provide emergency communication during times of crisis or disaster.

Question 2. When can an amateur radio operator transmit without identifying themselves in the air?

Option A: The transmitting signals to operate the model craft

Option B: The transmitted power is below 1 watt.

Option C: The transmissions are unmodulated.

Option D: The transmissions are short for making station adjustments.

Option D allows for transmitting without identification but only for making quick station adjustments and not communicating with other stations.

Question 3. Who is responsible for designating the station control operator?

Option A: The FCC

Option B: The station licensee

Option C: The frequency coordinator

Option D: Any licensed operator

The answer is option B, which states that the station licensee is responsible for designating the station control operator. This does mean that the person who holds the license for the amateur radio station is responsible for ensuring that the station is operated according to the FCC rules.

Question 4. If the control operator of an amateur radio station is not the station licensee, who is responsible for ensuring operations at the station?

Option A: All licensed amateurs

Option B: The station licensee

Option C: The control operator

Option D: The station licensee and the control operator and

Option D states that the control operator and the station licensee are responsible for the proper station operation. While the control operator is responsible for the immediate operation of the station and ensuring that it complies with the rules and regulations, the station licensee is ultimately responsible for the proper operation of the station.

Question 5. In the absence of documentation to the contrary in station records, who does the FCC assume to be the control operator?

Option A: The station custodian

Option B: The third-party participant

Option C: The person operating the station equipment

Option D: The station licensee

The answer is option D, which states that the FCC presumes the station licensee is the control operator of a ham radio station unless documentation is present in the station records.

Question 6. Which computer should the sound card port be connected to a transceiver's headphone or speaker output for operating digital modes?

Option A: Headphone output

Option B: Mute

Option C: Microphone or line input

Option D: PCI or SDI)

The answer is option A, which states that the headphone output of a transceiver should be connected to the sound card port of a computer for operating digital modes. Digital modes are a type of communication mode in amateur radio that allow operators to send and receive data using a computer and a transceiver.

Question 7. What could be the main component responsible for generating gain in an RF power amplifier?

Option A: Transformer

Option B: Transistor

Option C: Reactor

Option D: Resistor

The answer is option B, which states that a transistor could be the primary gain-producing component in an RF power amplifier. An RF power amplifier is an electronic device used to increase the power of a radio frequency signal. It comprises several components, including the input and output matching networks, coupling capacitors, and the transistor amplifier.

Question 8. Who defines the grounding requirements for an amateur radio antenna or tower among the following options?

Option A: FCC Part 97 Rules

Option B: Local electrical codes

Option C: FAA tower lighting regulations

Option D: UL recommended practices

The answer is option A, which states that the FCC Part 97 rules establish grounding requirements for amateur radio towers or antennas. The FCC (Federal Communications Commission) is the regulatory agency overseeing all radio communications in the United States, including amateur radio.

Question 9. What does the term "NCS" refer to in net operation?

Option A: Nominal Control System

Option B: Net Control Station

Option C: National Communications Standard

Option D: Normal Communications Syntax

The answer is option B, which states that "NCS" stands for Net Control Station in net operation. In amateur radio, a net is a formal on-air gathering of radio operators for a specific purpose, such as exchanging information, providing emergency communications support, or conducting training exercises. The Net Control Station (NCS) is the designated operator responsible for the organization and management of the net.

Question 10. What is the increase in power, measured in decibels (dB), when the power output is increased from 20 watts to 200 watts?

Option A: 10 dB

Option B: 12 dB

Option C: 18 dB

Option D: 28 dB

The answer is option A, which states that the increase in power is 10 dB. Decibel (dB) expresses power or gain in electronic circuits. When the power output is increased from 20 watts to 200 watts, the increase in power is calculated as follows:

Power gain in dB = 10 log (P2/P1)

P1 is the initial power output, and P2 is the final output.

In this case, P1 is 20 watts, and P2 is 200 watts. Plugging these values into the above formula, we get:

A power gain in dB = 10 logs (200/20)

= 10 logs (10)

= 10 x 1

= 10 dB

Therefore, the power output has increased by 10 dB.

Question 11. What electronic device shields other circuit components from excessive current flow?

Option A: Fuse

Option B: Capacitor

Option C: Inductor

Option D: All of these choices are correct

The correct answer is option A, which indicates that a fuse is an electronic device that protects other circuit components from overcurrent situations. A fuse is designed to protect other components in a circuit from excessive current. It is a small wire or filament that melts current more than the required value and flows through it, breaking the circuit and preventing further damage to other components.

Question 12. What is the standard sideband for single-sideband communication on 10-meter HF, VHF, and UHF frequencies?

Option A: Upper sideband

Option B: Lower sideband

Option C: Suppressed sideband

Option D: Inverted sideband

The correct answer is option A, which indicates that the upper sideband is typically used for single-sideband communication on 10-meter HF, VHF, and UHF frequencies. Single sideband (SSB) is a type of modulation used in radio communication that uses less bandwidth than traditional amplitude modulation (AM). In SSB, only one sideband and the carrier signal are transmitted, reducing the bandwidth required.

Question 13. What characteristic of a radio wave is used to define its polarization?

Option A: The orientation of the electric field

Option B: The orientation of the magnetic field

Option C: The ratio of energy in the magnetic field to the energy in the electric field

Option D: The ratio of the velocity to the wavelength

The answer is A - the orientation of the electric field. Radio waves are electromagnetic waves that consist of oscillating electric and magnetic fields. Polarization is a property of these fields, and it refers to the orientation of the electric field relative to the Earth's surface.

Question 14. What is the typical antenna polarization for making long-distance weak-signal CW and SSB contacts on the VHF and UHF bands?

Option A: Right-hand circular

Option B: Left-hand circular

Option C: Horizontal

Option D: Vertical

The typical antenna polarization used for long-distance weak-signal CW and SSB contacts on the VHF and UHF bands is horizontal. This is because most terrestrial communication on these bands is achieved through line-of-sight propagation, and horizontal polarization provides the best radiation pattern for this type of propagation

Question 15. What is an amateur radio station that facilitates the connection of other amateur stations to the internet called?

Option A: Gateway

Option B: Repeater

Option C: Digipeater

Option D: Beacon

The term given to an amateur radio station that connects other amateur stations to the internet is "gateway." Gateways often provide access to internet-based systems such as Echo Link, IRLP (Internet Radio Linking Project), and All Star. Gateways can be operated using various modes, such as FM, SSB, or digital modes, and can be located anywhere in the world. When an amateur station connects to a gateway, it can communicate with other amateur radio stations and internet users.

Chapter 7: Ham Radio for Preppers

Several forums, videos, and online purchases show that there are not only outdoor freaks who want to spend their free time with bushcraft, urban, survival, preppers, or similar. In the meantime, people are rethinking. For political and governmental reasons, fears but also ideas arise. For example, with those who prepare for the "worst case." What happens if the rule of law collapses? The infrastructure goes out and looting occur.

For such and other cases, some people arm themselves. At home with provisions or on the go with a backpack and the essentials to survive. The latter attracts more community interest due to the spirit of adventure. There has been "survival training" for years, which many people voluntarily book on vacation or at the weekend.

No matter how libertarian you stand for and whatever your vision of government power, someone has to regulate the spectrum, or it would be completely unnecessary, with potential users jamming each other left and right. Each developed country has a government agency that allocates radio spectrum for different uses, and in turn, the countries cooperate internationally through various treaties and agreements.

In the United States, this responsibility has been delegated by Congress to the Federal Communications Commission (FCC). Aside from the constitutionally questionable nature of such a delegation, this is the legal reality. The FCC issues licenses to people that allow them to use different parts of the radio spectrum for different purposes, such as radio and television broadcasting, public safety, mobile phones, the military, etc. Generally, you cannot do any radio transmission without a license. Some parts of the spectrum are available for the public to use for personal communication, and I will discuss them later in this article.

If we experience a total collapse of the rule of law, much of that could go away (with the National Firearms Act, for that matter). However, radio communication requires practice to be useful in an emergency, and you are much more likely to need your radio equipment in a situation that does not result in complete social disruption. As a result, it helps to know the rules, at least in general terms, and to have a plan for communicating within them.

Prepping For Emergencies

Radio was only a hobby of predominantly technically interested men for a long time, which received little attention. Since the introduction of cheap, worldwide means of communication, the spread of amateur radio has declined. However, the sales figures for radios have been increasing again for several years, especially since the Corona crisis. Why is that? Were many looking for a new hobby for the lockdown, or would you like to prepare much more for an expected crisis? Much points to the latter.

Actual amateur radio is a complex hobby. After you have acquired a license through an examination and received an official radio identification, you can get started. This is regulated worldwide. Licensed amateur radio operators can operate worldwide on various frequency bands, from shortwaves to decimeter waves. Setting up a system and exhausting the technical possibilities is essential to the job. Ultimately, however, the goal is communication with other amateur radio operators worldwide. This is where a phenomenon known as "DXing" comes to the rescue. Radio waves can reflect off the ionosphere under the right weather conditions. This way, you can reach the other side of the world, even with a not particularly powerful system.

Is The Old CB Radio Coming Back?

However, said the increase in radio equipment sales primarily affects CB radio. This stands for "citizens band radio" and is a license-free radio application for everyone. Before the advent of cell phones, there was a real CB boom. It was popular to have a radio in the car or truck. But many also had a base station at home. The technology worked on specified channels in the 27 MHz range and was previously intended primarily for short-range communication. In principle, however, large ranges can also be achieved with CB. Geographical altitude, a clear field of view, and a decent antenna are more important than mere performance regarding radio.

Preppers Recommend Cb Radio

Much suggests that hobby is not the main motivation for many new radio operators. Especially in the prepper scene, it is recommended to get a radio. Preppers are people who prepare for disaster scenarios. Before starting the Corona state of emergency, they were often dismissed as cranks or denigrated as "right-wing extremists" and "conspiracy theorists." Hardly anyone does that now. Preppers recommend CB radio because the technology is cheap and easy to understand. CB channel three is considered the preppers' unofficial emergency channel. You should listen to channel three every three hours in an emergency for three minutes.

Only radio is always reliable

There's a reason all armed forces worldwide are equipped with radios. In an emergency, you can only rely on equipment that you can completely control yourself. The "cyber pandemic" predicted by Klaus Schwab could soon paralyze the entire electronic infrastructure. Recently, cyber-attacks on municipal systems have increased So you can no longer rely on the Internet and telephone networks, which have long gone digital. In an emergency, your radio system and the battery are the only guaranteed means of communication.

In the past, it was not uncommon for amateur radio to be banned during the war. In recent years, it has also become increasingly common for regimes to cut off the Internet and telephones of citizens when there are protests or uprising movements so that the opposition cannot organize themselves. This has just happened in Cuba, for example. In such a situation, radio is the only way to keep in touch with others and spread messages. A little joke on the side: In theory, everyone can listen in on the radio, but probably due to the current surveillance mania of the globalists, a radio conversation is much more private than a message on Facebook or WhatsApp or a normal telephone call.

Radio Survival Kit

What's in my radio survival kit? This may seem redundant to most, but if you've spent a certain amount of time turning the tuning knob, it's highly appropriate to be able to easily make inquiries about what you hear or quickly tune in to what you want to listen to.

1. Reference material for inexperienced radio amateurs or people who are completely inexperienced in matters of radio communications. Description of the radio communication plan "3-3-3" phonetic alphabet telegraphic alphabet Q codes RST reports

2. List of key survivalist frequencies.

3. Unlicensed VHF frequencies, including channel numbers in our radio models belonging to permissible power common name note, e.g., "local chatter"

4. CB and Free band frequencies, including frequency type of radiation - FM, AM, USB, LSB channel type (CB, Free band, RC) channel name note, e.g., "emergency".

5. Local Scanner Frequencies, including details for radio programming if required. The list should include as many service frequencies as possible: in all local cities, police, fire, and public services, as well as the neighboring district, if close to the border of districts, all district services for this district and neighboring all local airport frequencies,

including ATIS and controllers full list of transitional (Itinerant) frequencies

6. Scanner frequencies across the region, traffic police, emergency services, and others.

7. National Engagement Frequencies listed in the National Field Engagement Guide, NIFOG.

8. Amateur radio by country (well, yes, this is purely for radio amateurs, but it does not hurt), including prefix the name of the country azimuths along the short and long paths distance latitude and longitude continent CQ zone

9. Coast Guard weather stations, their schedules, and frequencies. Time and frequency of broadcasts of all-weather informants. They is usually used by yachtsmen but affects a large area of the continental part and coastal areas. This is a great source of weather information when the local forecast is not on the air, or you can't hear it. Boston/NMF, Pt. Reyes/NMC, New Orleans/NMG, Kodiak/NOJ, Honolulu/KVM70

10. A complete list of marine VHF frequencies (check that you have a complete, international list), including channel number (1, 01A, 5, 05A) ship frequency frequency of reception on the common ship use

11. 11. Full list of NWS weather channels name or number frequently location if used within 2,000 km of you

12. Marine radiotelephone channels on all bands, including simplex and emergency. 4, 6, 8, 12, 16, 18/19, 22 and 22/26 MHz

13. Radio frequently bands allocated to radio amateurs (band plan). 160, 80, 60, 40, 20, 17, 15, 12, 10, 6, 2, 1.25 meters, 70, and 23 centimeters

14. Broadcast radio stations in your area in AM within 1000 km frequently distance azimuth city and region format (news, music, local, etc.)

15. Broadcast radio stations in your area in FM within 500 km callsign frequency distance azimuth city and region format (news, music, local, etc.)

16. Radio amateur repeaters within 300 km, on 10, 6, 2 meters, 220 and 430 MHz transmission frequency reception frequency subtone/subcode callsign location description

17. Table of signals with flags (international alphabet, phonetic alphabet, flag telegraph, and semaphore alphabet)

18. Equipment references (how to program your walkie-talkie to work with a repeater, set the receive-transmit difference, etc.)

19. Schemes for the construction of simple antennas and details of their structures J-pole simple Ground Plane on SO-239 multi-range dipole with coaxial and symmetrical feed line standard dipole lengths for common ranges inverted-vee length full wave loop ground plane simple antenna lengths for 1/4, 1/2 and full wave dipole at 160-2 meters

20. Assembly instructions for all antennas in your kit, lengths, adjustments, etc.

21. Time conversion table, UTC to local, to other time zones.

22. Radio frequency bands allocated to radio amateurs by the category (see 13)

23. Copies of radio documentation from amateur licensed bands, other

Conclusion

Congratulations on completing the "Ham Radio for Beginners" course! You have taken the first step towards exploring amateur radio's exciting and captivating world. This book has equipped you with the fundamental concepts of radio communication and an understanding of the equipment, regulations, and operating procedures required to become a licensed ham radio operator. However, this is only the beginning! As a ham radio operator, you can connect with people worldwide, engage in emergency communication, and even experiment with building your equipment. The hobby of amateur radio is both intriguing and rewarding, offering endless opportunities for enjoyment and learning. So why not leap and become a licensed ham radio operator? With the knowledge you've gained from this book, you're well on your way to unlocking a world of possibilities.

Remember, the key to success in this hobby is to keep learning and exploring. Join a local club, participate in contests, and communicate with other ham radio operators to share your experiences and knowledge. What are you waiting for? Get your license, grab your radio, and start exploring the fascinating world of ham radio!

References

http://www.arrl.org/what-is-ham-radio

https://www.itu.int/hub/2022/06/4u1itu-ham-radio-amateur-station-60-years/

https://fieldradio.org/how-far-can-a-ham-radio-reach/

https://uomustansiriyah.edu.iq/media/lectures/5/5_2019_02_03!06_16_46_PM.pdf

https://user.eng.umd.edu/~tretter/commlab/c6713slides/ch7.pdf

https://www.edaboard.com/threads/how-can-i-build-a-multiband-am-transmitter.398932/

https://www.whatdotheyknow.com/request/list_of_available_amateur_radio_2

https://www.westmountainradio.com/new-ham.php

http://www.arrl.org/Clubs/search/page:31/Tag.name:Digital%20Modes/model:Group

https://turbofuture.com/consumer-electronics/Ham-Radio-Lingo-Explained

https://www.fcc.gov/wireless/bureau-divisions/mobility-division/commercial-radio-operator-license-program/examinations

https://www.marinerslearningsystem.com/fcc-element-1-online-exam.html

https://www.mometrix.com/academy/ham-radio-technician-class

https://willowhavenoutdoor.com/what-is-the-best-ham-radio-for-preppers/

Ham Radio For Dummies By John Wiley (2021)

Made in the USA
Columbia, SC
16 March 2024

33136700R00061